THE
DONKEYMAN

Philip Allott

Published by Sigma Leisure – an imprint of
Sigma Press, 5 Alton Road, Wilmslow, Cheshire SK9 5DY, England.

British Library Cataloguing in Publication Data
A CIP record for this book is available from the British Library.

ISBN: 978-1-85058-845-0 (13-digit); 1-85058-845-7 (10-digit)

Typesetting and Design by: Sigma Press, Wilmslow, Cheshire.

Cover photograph: Knaresborough Donkey Farm, Harrogate Road, Knaresborough *(Yorkshire Post)*

Printed in Poland – Polskabook UK

Foreword
by the Rt Hon Ann Widdecombe MP

The bus pass generation will remember its donkey years and those holidays long ago when we went not to Spain or Greece but to the English seaside. Down we ran to the beach with our buckets and spades and, of course, our sixpences which would buy a donkey ride or our shillings which would buy both the ride and an ice cream.

Oh, those donkey rides! What fun when they trotted and we thought we were galloping, pretending we were riding Champion the Wonder Horse. Yet I doubt if we took much notice of the donkey man. He was just there to collect the sixpences and make the donkeys go.

This book recreates vividly an occupation about which very little is genuinely known and is a splendid evocation of an age which has vanished but is not yet too distant. Animal lovers and historians alike will just adore it while the general reader will find an intriguing insight into a changing twentieth-century scene.

How did donkeys get their names? What happened to them in the winter? How were their feet protected, their harnesses serviced? How did the owner and his family live? And, oh dear, what happened when the donkeys could no longer work?

This book is not just about the man and his beasts but also about the social milieu in which he worked: the vagrant, the village idiot, the policing, the social club. Yet it is still the character of the donkeyman which gives the book its life. In a less politically correct age he devised his own system of dealing with nuisances and was assisted rather than restrained in his efforts.

The author has a sharp eye for the absurd and eccentric as well as fond memories of his father. The detail is captivating, sometimes charming and sometimes shocking but never dull.

Written in a light but literate style, this is a book for all ages.

Ann Widdecombe

Preface

The medieval market town of Knaresborough sits on the edge of the scenic River Nidd. Its dramatic river setting can be found on countless picture postcards, thanks to its world-famous viaduct. The town is also famous for its historical characters, such as: St Robert the hermit; John Metcalf, a blind road builder; and Mother Shipton, the prophetess. What is less known is that the town continued over the years to be the home of may other characters, who one might politely call local eccentrics.

One of these was my father David Allott, known locally as The Donkeyman or Donkey Dave. Father was given these nicknames on account of the large brood of donkeys he reared, gave rides with at the side of the River Nidd and also took to donkey derby fund-raising events until his death in 1993.

In the small town of Knaresborough, which expanded in the late 1960s, father was a familiar figure and in summer would be seen working his donkeys or standing on the High Bridge chatting to both locals and tourists. His donkeys, through their fund-raising activities for charities and the like, became famous throughout the North of England. Father had by far the largest number of donkeys in the region, which he loved and cherished – often, it was said, more than his relatives.

He saw himself as a normal person working hard to support his family. But he was often seen as something else by those who were kept awake on account of his donkeys' braying, those who fell in the donkey droppings left on Knaresborough's roads, or those that were occasionally hit by father because of their 'lippiness'. Despite his unusual and somewhat eccentric behaviour, however, he had a profound sense of justice and a belief in fair play. He would on occasions stand up to the authorities and sometimes cause them acute embarrassment, when he believed they were wrong.

How my father made a living, how he started, the various adventures that took place and how it all ended are the subjects of this book. Most of the events portrayed in this book actually took place, although to make the book easier to read a number of them have been grouped together and in some cases developed. I hope you enjoy reading it as much as I did writing it.

Philip D. Allott

Acknowledgements

I would like to thank the following people for helping with the writing, editing and marketing of this book:

Rt. Hon Ann Widdecombe MP for writing the Foreword; Katherine Cox for her editorial help and input; Raymond Allott for his editorial help and input; Matthew Allott for helping with the contents; Kirsty Allott for her patience in proof reading and copywriting; Tony Francis for his editorial editing expertise; Sandra MacGregor for reading the draft copy and words of encouragement. Beverley, Hannah and Gary Allison for the final proof reading.

I also thank the following people and organisations for their cooperation and/or contributions:

Miss EG Adamson; BBC Look North; Mrs Linda Blackburn; Mr Peter Brear; Mr Jim Brook; Mr Paul Doolan; Mrs Eileen Ferguson; Dr Arnold Kellett; Les & Trina Hall; Mr & Mrs Tim Harris; Mr Kevin Halstead; Mr Edward Harrower; Harrogate Advertiser; Huddersfield Examiner; Knaresborough Post; Mrs Margaret Knight; Mr & Mrs Charlie & Mary Roberts; Mrs Rosemary Mills; Mrs Margaret McCollom; York Press; Yorkshire Post; Yorkshire Evening Post; Miss Becky Ray; Mr Sheppard; Mandy Simmons; Mrs Margaret Wood; Mrs Janet Woodhead; Radio York.

To my wife, Sandra

Contents

Prologue

The height of the business

The year was 1967, and Britain was enjoying a warmish, mid-August Sunday afternoon after a wet start to the holiday season. Frank Sinatra's 'Strangers in the Night' had just been made record of the year and Israel had, in June, fought the Six-Day War. In England, large numbers of people still spent their holidays at home in the UK and everyone was determined to enjoy the remainder of the summer in the best way they could.

In the historic town of Knaresborough, day-trippers mingled with those staying at local guest houses and nearby campsites, as well as with the local population. In those days, only tourist shops, cafés and the town's visitor attractions such as the Castle and Mother Shipton's estate and cave were open. Visitors flocked over the High Bridge to reach Mother Shipton's attractions in such large numbers that they would stop the traffic; a sole police officer would try in vain to direct people and cars out of the large car park, which was based on the river's edge at Conyngham Hall.

David with his donkeys

On the other side of the river to the car park was the entrance to Bilton Fields. An ice cream van was parked in between two large wooden gates and a small queue had developed to purchase its wares. Hung on the fence adjoining the wooden gates were two scuffed hand-painted boards, with red writing on a yellow background, simply stating 'Donkey Rides'.

Visitors and locals venturing through the second set of wooden gates arrived in Bilton Fields, which ultimately led to Harrogate; although few of the visitors who walked through had the stamina to cover the four-mile distance.

Looking down through the gates a children's miniature roundabout with a large, bright, multi-coloured umbrella could be seen a few feet away. Further down the first field a line-up of six donkeys faced a yellow wooden seat, on which sat four scruffy youths of varying ages.

Each of the donkeys facing the youths was kitted out in the same harness. This comprised a dark saddle, an upright, bright red, bucket handle for a child to hold, and leather stirrups, but without the normal accompanying metal irons used by a rider to mount and dismount. A red bell collar with four Victorian bells hung round each donkey's neck, along with a red and black bridle, which bore an individual name for each animal. Each bridle had studs and bright brass or silver buckles.

Donkey rides cost a tanner (2½ pence) and those paying the fare were led at a slow speed by one of the youths along the footpath by the riverside, past three council park benches and back again. Intermittently, queues of adults with young children built up around the donkeys and every so often a voice would boom out "mind your backs". The voice belonged to a middle-aged, clean-shaven man wearing a yellow button-up smock, brown boots and a tatty

The donkeys were lead slowly in twos along the riverside. The more intelligent donkeys would go very slowly to avoid having to give too many rides!

leather moneybag. This man was David Allott, my father, who for nearly forty years was to dominate the Knaresborough riverside scene, every summer.

The business opened at 1.30pm and continued on a Sunday until either rain intervened or St John's Parish Church bells rang, announcing evening service at around 6pm. On other days, during school holidays the business pottered along much the same, although closing time was generally around 5pm.

Saturdays were nearly always reserved for donkey racing, as this generated far more money. In 1967 the donkeys attended a number of events in the North of England including Manchester, Leeds, Harrogate and Wakefield.

On a Sunday, in-between bouts of collecting money – often to fund a few beers – father would leave the donkeys in the care of one of the scruffy youths. This allowed him time to stand on the High Bridge and chat to strangers or drink in the George Hotel, now renamed the Yorkshire Lass, or at the World's End at the other end of the High Bridge.

Pubs in those days closed early on a Sunday and did not open until 7pm so to get round this minor technical problem, those in the know, including my father, would visit a place called Uncle Tom's Cabin, based on Waterside. Here the then owner of the restaurant was more than happy to sell beer to trusted locals.

Due to rising overheads the cost of rides was increased in 1970 to 5^d (2p in today's money). Some customers were so disgruntled that they refused to pay.

During rainy periods the donkeys were placed under the trees in Bilton fields

After top-up drinking and possibly by now semi-inebriated, he would return to the donkeys and then try to organise the lads, along with the donkeys, who during his absence had generally gone wayward. At the end of the riding session, the donkeys were walked back up to the Harrogate Road field, where they had their harnesses removed and were afterwards allowed to graze.

From 1967 onwards, an old caravan in the field provided a brief refuge for the donkey boys who, after helping with the animals, were given potted beef sandwiches before being driven at a rather slow and often wobbly speed home to the Broadacres Council Estate.

Welcome to my father's world!

Chapter 1

A Donkeyman in the Making

David Walter Allott was born in 1927 at Denby Farm, Darrington, three miles from Pontefract, West Yorkshire. The family moved shortly after his birth to Starbeck, a suburb of Harrogate, following my grandfather's appointment to a minor executive post with the West Yorkshire Road Car Company, the local bus operator. They lived in a comfortable, semi-detached house in close proximity to the railway crossing and, despite the harshness of the recession, my father seems to have had a reasonable, if modest, childhood.

Times were tough in the great depression of the 1930s and unemployment and poverty were rife. My grandfather earned £2 10s (£2.50) a week which, after his house rent of 15 shillings (75 pence), left him the equivalent of £1.75 in today's money for the family to live on. Unable to manage on the limited money he earned, my grandfather decided to confront his boss over his pay, to try and secure an increase. This was a rather bold thing to do in 1931 and was nearly his undoing. Grandfather's boss asked a pay clerk to bring in the company's wage records. On examination it was discovered that my grandfather was being over-paid by half a crown (25 pence) a week. Grandfather was not only refused a pay rise but had his salary cut by half a crown. Afraid to leave, grandfather had to endure the situation, although my father later recalled that there was no annual summer holiday that year.

The family, comprising my grandfather Cyril, my grandmother Edwena, father's sister Margaret and father normally had a week's summer holiday in Whitby. It was during these breaks that he learned the rudiments of donkey-keeping. At that time, donkeys were kept largely by gypsies. Grandfather, conscious of his position in society as a parson's grandson, had banned my father from even speaking to the travellers. Father once enquired about gypsies after one had asked my grandfather for a match, and he was politely but firmly told that these were poor people who could not afford a house.

In Whitby, however, he was allowed to assist with the donkeys because they were owned by the Fortune family, whose descendants to this day are world-famous for their kipper curing business. This was due to the fact that the Fortunes were God-fearing folk and devoted Quakers. Grandfather, who had also been brought up in a strict religious household (and also did not like gypsies who often operated seaside donkeys),

This picture shows David's friend William Fortune, aged 74, putting out his herrings for smoking

had no problem allowing his young son to assist the Fortunes with their donkeys.

The donkeys gave rides on the beach, tide permitting, and did so every day of the week except on Sunday. From all accounts, my father 'Young Dave' spent almost his entire holiday with William (Willie) Fortune, who was some years older than father and through this work his love of the donkey trade was born. His duties included saddling up, moving the donkeys down to the beach, leading them along to give rides and even strapping their nosebags on at lunchtime. The donkeys were kept in a field near the church and abbey, located in the old town. Given the geography of Whitby with its many hills, it must have been a very tiring day for a youngster, just leading the donkeys back and forth from the field, let alone assisting with beach rides. Whether he earned any money from his seaside holiday hobby no one knows, although we do know that he greatly enjoyed it and became lifelong friends with almost the entire Fortune family. This experience was to stand him in excellent stead when he launched his own donkey business in the 1950s.

Father failed the 11 plus and his education therefore took place exclusively at Starbeck School, which is today a primary school. By contrast, his sister Margaret, who was a few years younger, passed the examination with flying colours; she went to Knaresborough Grammar School and later studied at a teacher training college. The issue of who attended which school clearly played heavily on his mind, and he still spoke about it with an air of frustration, even in his fifties. By all accounts Starbeck School was a tough place and it was not uncommon for pupils to be caned for truancy in front of the whole school.

He secured his first farming job with Mr and Mrs Bellerby and left school at 14, without a certificate to his name. Unlike his own father, who had learnt farming as a leisurely fee-paying farm pupil, my father had to work hard to gain his knowledge and was sent to lodge on a farm at Killinghall, located just a few miles away from his parents' home. He developed a habit of changing farms annually in order to learn new agricultural techniques. Life on these farms was tough in war-torn Britain and he used to tell some grisly tales in later life.

On one particular farm, ham was kept in the house loft and could easily develop maggots. One old farm worker thought the maggots actually improved the quality of the ham and would refuse to eat the meat unless it contained them. I have often thought about what this maggot-ridden ham must have tasted like!

Pre-wartime, farm machinery was horse-powered and the equipment used by the horses, according to father, was often very old. He liked the stock aspect of farming but was not too keen on the arable side of the business. After moving from farm to farm, he ended up working for the

West Riding War Agricultural Executive Committee, which was nicknamed by those who worked for it as the WAR-RAG. This organisation was tasked during the Second World War with claiming back surplus land for crop growing – including the 200-acre Stray, a public open space in Harrogate, old coal sites and, where appropri-

This picture was taken during one of the family's trips to Whitby. The donkeys were owned by the Fortune family, who owing to their staunch religious views did not work on a Sunday. Father spent most of his holiday helping with the donkeys. The lady in the picture is believed to be his Grandmother Barber.

ate, assisting bigger farms to increase their food yields through mechanisation.

My grandfather had, earlier in the war, been appointed machinery officer. By all accounts this was a senior position in which he had a large number of people reporting to him. Father joined as a tractor driver/helping hand and was posted to Aberford, West Yorkshire. Aberford is a small village that runs parallel with the A1(M) and is a picturesque place with a river, pubs and fish and chip shop. In those days it was an important part of the government's drive in the North of England to improve farming efficiency.

Father was required to lodge in the village with another young chap, in order to be on top of the job. In later life he complained that he would have liked to have been in the Army but farming was a reserved occupation and there seems to be little evidence that he actually bothered to pursue any military ambitions. There is even some anecdotal information that my grandmother put pressure on her husband to pull a few strings to ensure that father did not get posted to the Army.

One ambition he did have, however, was courting and with the use of an old motorcycle, he became a regular figure on the Leeds dance floors. Dancing in those days was very much a contact activity, although it would seem that dance halls were just as tough as some of today's night-clubs. In one incident he got into a fight with a man in the gents' toilets after telling the chap that his mother can't have given him many toys to play with when he was young! It was at one of these dances that he met Betty Anderson from Bond Street, Leeds – a meeting which was to change his life and create mine. My mother-to-be was only 16 when she met father and in later life he said that she had looked much older.

After a few years of courting, father proposed to my mother, although this did not receive universal approval from his future in-laws. My maternal grandfather, Frank Anderson, objected to the proposed marriage and it was only when my mother reached twenty that he relented.

Relations between my father and his father-in-law remained strained for the remainder of Frank's life. On

Taken in the 1930s this picture shows the Allotts. This family comprised Cyril Allott, Edwena Allott, father David Allott and Margaret Allott. Note the formal pose in keeping with era.

the one hand, Frank thought that my father was not good enough for his daughter and on the other my father despised my grandfather for his small-minded ways. Certainly Frank Anderson never had a senior employment position in his life and moved between different caretaking jobs, although from my own limited knowledge he and my grandmother Alice, always seemed happy.

It would also be fair to say that my father never came into his own in his senior appointments; he left the WAR-RAG around 1949 to take up employment as a yardman with a builders' material supplier, C. A. Nettleton & Co based at Dragon Road, Harrogate.

One thing that is clear from old family letters is that mother and father were deeply in love; my mother could not wait to get married so that she could move away from Leeds, to Bogs Lane, Starbeck. Mother actually

The picture was taken in 1952 outside the Holy Trinity Parish Church, Leeds. Left to right, Cryril & Edwena Allott, Gerald Walker, David and Betty, Margaret Allott, John Anderson, Frank and Alice Anderson.

thought that the name was rather romantic in those days, and it was only years later that 'bog' became associated with more negative concepts.

In 1952 mother and father were married at the Holy Trinity Parish Church in Leeds. Looking at the marriage certificate gives an interesting glimpse of everyone's status. My father is described as a yardman, mother a secretary, grandfather Allott a machinery officer (WRAC) and grandfather Anderson, a caretaker.

After a brief honeymoon in Blackpool, my parents settled down to married life in a caravan. Located in Bogs Lane, the caravan was on about five acres of land owned by Mrs Florence Todd. The site allowed my father, for the first time since the war, to also indulge in his passions for farming and animals. By late 1955, he recorded in his diary the following stock: three bullocks, one sow in pig, one sow with litter, two store pigs, three geese and one gander, thirty hens, three ferrets, four donkeys, a pony trap, seven saddles and six bridles.

The caravan itself was not a very grand affair and had neither piped water nor a bathroom. Cold water had to be carried by bucket from a tap 300 yards away and, looking back, times must have been rather hard. An attempt was made by my parents to have piped water connected in 1960, but Mrs Todd refused them permission, as she wanted my parents to secure accommodation elsewhere.

Placed at the entrance to a gated drive leading to Mrs Todd's bungalow, the caravan was a little dilapidated and had at least one broken window. However, to my mother and father this was their first home and both would hanker to go back to it in later life, with naïve nostalgia.

Father's job at Nettleton's consisted of unloading lorries and loading up both local builders' wagons and the firm's own vehicles. By all accounts it was a rather messy job and certainly

This was a family picture taken of David with his sister Margaret when he was around 20 years old.

tough on the back. Sometimes father would be required to accompany one of the firm's tradesmen and render assistance. It was through one of these jobs that he learnt how to be a chimney sweep, something that would eventually stand him in very good stead.

In the evenings father set about developing his own smallholding. This, although expensive, was relatively easy because the site at Bogs Lane came with a string of old chicken buildings and sheds that could easily be converted for other animals. Within a short time pigs, hens and a pony had all been purchased. The pigs were for breeding and eventual selling at auction, while the freshly laid eggs could be sold at the front entrance gate.

Early in 1954 father injured his back from all the heavy lifting he was required to do at Nettleton's and he was forced to rest in bed. Ultimately this resulted in a considerable amount of lost income and his departure from the firm. However, with the money my mother earned as a secretary with a Harrogate solicitor's practice, called Raworths, things were not all doom and gloom.

It was while lying in bed and feeling sorry for himself, that father decided to go it alone by giving donkey rides at the riverside in Knaresborough. To him this seemed a natural thing to do, but to his family and friends, it seemed a crazy idea.

Chapter 2

The Donkeys

Father was not a person for taking advice and anyone questioning the merits of the project was quickly dismissed by him. However, the biggest challenge was to persuade the then local Knaresborough Urban District Council (KUDC), to grant permission to use its land in Bilton Fields for giving rides.

Cyril David Leslie Allott, alias Grandfather Allott, had senior Masonic contacts and seemed the ideal front man to talk with the rather insular and by nature suspicious KUDC Officers. However, grandfather was a man more concerned with his local standing in society and he point-blank refused to co-operate. Nevertheless, father was not easily dissuaded and after a number of meetings with the Town Clerk, riverside donkey rides were finally agreed.

In 1955 he purchased three donkeys, saddled them up, tied them together and single-handedly took them down to Bilton Fields at the side of the River Nidd to give rides. The three donkeys – Punch, Judy and Muffin – had, by all accounts, a very hard time and so did father. The Bogs Lane smallholding was nearly two miles away and that distance had to be walked before any rides were even given.

The first Sunday was two weeks before Whitsuntide and the donkeys made twelve shillings and sixpence. The following week father put up a sign proclaiming the rides and takings increased to fifty shillings. As he was to joke later, it pays to advertise. In preparation for the coming Whit Sunday, he purchased another donkey for two pounds, ten shillings. He recalled many years later that the Bank Holiday Sunday had netted him £10. Not bad, he said, when the average wage was just £7 per week.

Donkey riding by the River Nidd continued throughout Sundays and Bank Holidays during the summer almost without exception, until my mother's death in 1996.

Not long after the donkeys started providing rides in Bilton fields, father was approached by George Dobbie, who was then a well-known sports commentator and racing journalist. George asked father if he could bring along a few donkeys to a derby, which was being held at nearby Goldsborough, after one of the big race meetings. Although father did not have sufficient donkeys to supply them all, he had enough animals when they were pooled with other providers to meet George's requirements.

In the 1950s, donkey derbies were often held in an evening after race meetings, in order to extend the racing day. The jockeys who rode the donkeys at these events were all professionals who, in many cases, had ridden earlier in the day. Charlie Roberts, who was one of these professionals, estimated that a donkey derby at Wetherby attracted over 3,000 spectators and, presumably, many of these would have attended the race day earlier. Within the matter of a few years, father was taking his donkeys to a large number of post-race meetings, as evening jobs. To lock out other suppliers, he started borrowing donkeys

In 1955, father also gave rides using a trotting pony called Dolly – Father with Dolly and one of the donkey helpers

from other owners (see chapter 6) which soon enabled him to be the exclusive provider and, more importantly able to command a higher fee.

At the start of the business, management of the donkeys was co-ordinated from the Bogs Lane smallholding, which was split into a number of sections. Access to the site was gained by a small lane that ran from the roadside parallel to the side of Allen Brothers pig farm to Mrs Todd's bungalow at the bottom of the field. The land above the bungalow and to its right was let to my father. This gave him the majority of the site, including the former apple orchard, although a limited number of other people also had access rights.

Mrs Todd lived in a post-war asbestos prefabricated building that was adjacent to a number of wooden sheds. Many number of these buildings had been put up by Mr Todd, a chicken farmer who had died in the 1950s. The sheds were let out to a variety of characters. One of these

The jockeys who rode the donkeys in the 1950s were all professionals

people was Fred Hawks, a First World War veteran who repaired Singer sewing machines and became a great friend of my father's. Fred would often help him with the painting of harnesses and pre-preparation work.

Much of the harness used with the donkeys was either made by father or modified from surplus equipment. A central theme that drew attention to the donkeys was a bright collar made up by father from surplus leather and painted red. It contained four brass or silver bells, which each animal had to wear. Even today the sound of fast ringing small bells causes my heart to flutter, in anticipation of a donkey having just broken loose and in possible danger.

Other items of harness included a bridle, with the donkey's name written on the front and a saddle with a handle, made from one taken off a bucket. Many of the saddles were purchased in a poor state of repair, often with ripped leather and sometimes broken 'trees' or 'frames'. From 1955 onwards, he would work throughout the winter re-building and sometimes even re-covering the saddles with fresh leather. I hesitate to say 'new' leather because hardly anything was ever new in his world, although in fairness he became – following much practice – a skilled saddler. Nearly every saddle that passed through his hands was also modified to accommodate a red handle.

Work on the harness was carried out in the 'saddle room' as father rather grandly called it. In truth it was a 1920s red single-decker bus which now rested on a number of old wooden railway sleepers. Nettles protruded from underneath the shell and access was gained via a small wooden door located at the rear of the body.

Although the engine had long since been removed, various artefacts from its former life on the roads still remained. These included wooden grab handles, overhead luggage containers and some kind of display cabinet at the front of the bus for showing the final destination.

The bus body was fitted out with saddle and bridle racks. The bell collars were placed vertically on old cotton bobbins under the bridles. The whole saddle room stank of a sickly smelling substance called neatsfoot oil. This rather foul white fatty substance was stored outside in a wooden barrel and had been purchased from a local butcher, who had accumulated the oil by melting down pigs' trotters! Father and his helpers would take small scoops of the fat from the barrel, melt it over a paraffin heater and work it into the underside of the leather, using an old paintbrush, to both preserve it and add suppleness.

The saddle room also contained various medicines for the donkeys as well as paints for putting names on to the bridles and colouring the saddle handles and bell collars. Leather-working tools were also kept in the shed along with anything else to be hidden from my mother!

It was important to father that the equipment used on the donkeys replicated that used at the seaside and he would often go to great lengths to purchase items that matched, and also to find more donkeys. This required him to travel to horse fairs all over the North of England and deal with people, gypsies and others, who were often more eccentric than himself. The fairs took place at Yarm, Appleby, Topcliffe and Boroughbridge and included much horse trotting and the selling of equipment, along with very heavy drinking. The most exciting of these fairs was Yarm, which father would sometimes camp out at, as explained in chapter 15.

Although donkey riding generated an income for father it was a very seasonally-based occupation and depended on the weather at least being reasonable. His main source of income was to be generated from donkey derbies, although that really did not get going until the mid 1960s.

Around 1957 father's drinking became quite serious after he and my mother lost their first child, Alice, at birth and were advised not to try for more. Further tragedy struck in 1958 when a faulty oil heater used for keeping hens warm, caught fire, destroying many of the farm animals and gutting nearly all the sheds. Having no water hydrants nearby contributed to the disaster, with the local fire brigade tenders, called to fight the blaze, quickly running dry. By the end of the day much of the stock had either perished or had to be humanely destroyed, and none of it had been insured. The psychological impact all this had on my father

Some of the first people to ride on the donkeys were Janet and Trevor Dawson from Leeds. The picture was taken in 1954 – the young boy does not have any socks on after an accident at the Knaresborough paddling pool.

is difficult to judge, although I am told that his moodiness and awkwardness with people reached an all-time high.

At around this time, one of his friends, Jack Barrass, came to the rescue. Jack was a tough, old-fashioned farmer who in those days had a farm tenancy at Plumpton, near Knaresborough. By manipulating his own employer, Jack was able to help father by providing him with some pigs and hens, thus enabling him to attempt a fresh start. This friendly gesture was periodically repeated with tools and various other items for the next thirty years. Why Jack chose to help is difficult to say. Father said it was because he saw him as the son he never had. However, whatever the motive, the pair became extremely close and Jack eventually became my godfather.

As a consequence of the fire my father concentrated more on his donkeys and it was these that consistently occupied his time until his death more than three decades later.

By early 1959, father's work had five core activities: farming, chimney sweeping, donkey riding, cattle-droving for a sometimes drunken Irish dealer called Frank Kelly, and helping out at the various local livestock auctions. Father led a tough life, which was marred by bouts of heavy drinking, especially with Kelly.

On December 22nd 1959, three days before Christmas, I was eventually born after a troublesome labour. Father said I had been born to run the donkeys, although my mother and I would always dispute this. He celebrated my birth by going into every pub in Knaresborough and purchasing drinks all round. A number of people can still remember this event and it must have been a very heavy night.

Chapter 3

Earliest Recollections

Home, for the first two years of my life, was the old-fashioned wooden caravan still located at the top of Mrs Todd's drive. My own bedroom had a cracked black-painted window, and further down the caravan was my parents' bedroom, half-shielded by a heavy velvet curtain. The caravan had a slight food smell which, looking back, I recall being reassuring.

Life continued to be incredibly hard for my parents, although I believe they were happier then than in later life. Father earned additional money from chimney sweeping, a trade he had learned at Nettleton's. Always slightly eccentric, even when he was relatively young, his chosen attire for sweeping work was an old suit. Working days always started with my father giving me a kiss as he left the caravan to go sweeping. Although at the time I was only two, I can still recall even today, that his clothing smelt of burnt soot.

Part of my own day was taken up with feeding the mismatched selection of bantams and hens, which gathered at the foot of the caravan. At the age of only two, my skills with throwing were not well developed and most of the corn slipped through the steps I was sitting on. Donkeys were allowed to roam freely up to the caravan, as were other animals, which were all categorised by my parents as either 'hostile' or 'friendly'.

One animal, a droving dog called Roy, acted as my bodyguard; anyone, or anything, apart from my parents, who ventured in my way was prone to get a savage nip as Mrs Todd, the landowner, one day found out.

Father had decided to take Roy away on one of his frequent cattle-moving jobs and Judy, a motherly sort of donkey, was bridled up by my mother to provide me with rides. The donkey and I were left to our own devices. It was difficult for me to mount this relatively tall donkey so, after some consideration of the problem, I tried to use a cardboard box, which naturally collapsed. This brought howls of laughter from father on his return later in the day.

It was around this time that Punch, one of the donkeys, picked me up by my shirt and tried to drown me in a nearby water butt. The sight of a donkey stealing me, with mother in hot pursuit complete with rolling pin, must have proved highly entertaining for the adjacent roadside passers-by. However, it was less entertaining for poor Punch, because

The author gets a donkey ride on Daisy the donkey. Note the old bus body in the background which was used as the saddle room.

father called him a child snatcher and promptly sold him to a horse dealer. The idyllic summer of 1962 was abruptly broken when a letter arrived from the Harrogate Borough Council, that caused by father to flare into a rage. The Council, which had previously given my parents an annual licence (number M2) to put a caravan at Bogs Lane, had decided not to renew it. The Council, in its defence, quoted violations of the Town and Country Planning Act along with a number of related planning issues, such as not having any running water. This was potentially a serious problem and mother, forever a fighter, made an appointment along with father to see the appropriate Council officer.

In the 1950s Harrogate Borough Council administered local government management for the Harrogate area, which included Starbeck. Knaresborough had its own council, the KUDC referred to earlier. The Harrogate Council offices were at Crescent Gardens, Harrogate. The department charged with the matter was the Public Health department, which was under the direction of a male officer called Dodsworth.

Dodsworth's office was based on the first floor of Crescent Gardens. His window looked over a triangle of green land between the main road and the council complex which still today provides a protective buffer from ambitious developers.

Dodsworth was charged with resolving matters and it would seem from subsequent accounts he had little time for my parents. He told them they had to move and he would try to find them a suitable council house.

Father recalled many years later that he then asked Dodsworth what would happen if he did not move. Dodsworth said that after the current licence had expired, council workmen would pull the caravan on to the highway and my father would then be arrested by the police for obstruc-

Muffin, Jenny, Tiny and Punch. This picture was taken in 1960. After Punch tried to drown the
author he was sold off. Muffin, Jenny and Tiny continued in active service until the 1970s
when they became infirm. During this time Jenny gave birth to Rosy and Tiny to Jill. Muffin lost
his teeth through grinding wood and Jenny and Tiny became lame. Father had all three of
them put humanely to sleep at the Harrogate Road fields in 1974. Father was so upset
afterwards that he could not eat for days.

tion. He was not someone to be threatened and when he asked in an
aggressive voice what would happen to his wife and son, Dodsworth said
they could go to the Knaresborough Workhouse.

Father could contain himself no longer and he flew into a rage. He was
later to recall the precise words that he used: "The first bastard who
comes to move my caravan will have his head blown off and if necessary
the second. An Englishman's home is his castle and you have no right to
interfere with our home. As for you, you bastard, both you and this desk
can go out of the window now."

Father then picked up the heavy wooden desk and started to lift it
forwards towards the large council office window, with Dodsworth now
trapped and cowering behind it. It was only my mother's speedy intervention that saved the health officer from almost certain death.
Dodsworth rather sensibly never wrote to them again, although neither
of my parents were fools and both realised it was only a matter of time
before they would have to move.

The search for a new house went in fits and starts, with the 'Harrogate
Advertiser' being scanned carefully each week. After looking at a
number of unsatisfactory properties in Starbeck, my parents found a

house in Knaresborough. Buying in Knaresborough was preferable for a number of reasons. Firstly the council gave an up-front purchasing grant and, secondly, the property would be nearer the riverside. And last, but not least, a move to Knaresborough would take them away from any influence that the despised Harrogate Borough Council officials would be able to exert.

My parents' choice of property was located at Park Place, a two-bedroom (later converted to three), brick-built cottage within easy reach of the High Street. Park Place was an old-fashioned cobbled street which in those days had a jam factory on one side and the Roxy Cinema on the other. A low-level wall ran parallel to the front of the property, with an opening in the middle for pedestrians. It is said that the hole in the wall had been caused by the accidental impact of a Second World War tank. Even today the top of Park Place is known by the locals as 'the hole in the wall'.

The left-hand side of Park Place provided access to the back of some High Street shops, whilst on the right-side Winteringham Hall was located, later sadly to be demolished in favour of a small range of stereo-typical 1960s shops.

The property was for sale through Thornton and Linley, local auctioneers and estate agents who father knew well as a result of his cattle-droving work. In a rash decision, the manager at Thornton and Linley, added a further £100 to the £1,000 asking price, something father was still cursing him for some twenty years later!

After a couple of looks around the house, it was duly purchased and work began on its modernisation. The property had been owned by an elderly lady and required quite a lot of work. The first important item was a bathroom, which was created by reducing the space occupied by the main bedroom. Fortunately for my parents, a rather timely small legacy arrived from the death of a relative, whose kind gesture covered the bathroom's construction.

To say father was not very good at DIY is an understatement. Whilst he could fence, hedge and – to a limited degree – engineer, his skills for neat, patient decorating were almost nil. My recollections of his early plaster filling projects for example were, to say the least, messy. The truth was that decorating and house repairs were not his forte and as time progressed mother took up the slack he left.

The decorating of Park Place was undertaken by an assortment of people including my paternal grandfather, Edgar Shepherd and some of the donkey boys. By late spring the house was ready for occupation, despite there remaining a range of defects, including a leaky roof. However, this was the family's exciting new home and after a few furniture trips in the back of father's large van, we had moved in.

Chapter 4

Hospitals

A few weeks after the move something happened which was so traumatic that it was to change the family's life forever. In the new house, the telephone dominated the living-room. It was one of those black Bakelite units, with a little drawer underneath that housed a list of popular phone numbers. Unfortunately like many things at Park Place, it was also covered in dust. One fateful day it rang and my mother spoke softly into the handset before pausing and then speaking again. Her voice became emotional and she started to cry.

She put down the receiver and started to cuddle me. In direct contrast to my father, mother had always been warm and reassuring. This time however, she wanted reassurance from me, not something always easy to grasp when you're only three. My mother spoke in a soft whisper: "It's your father," she began. "He's been involved in a road accident and has lost a lot of blood, they're not sure at the hospital if he is going to last the night."

Mother was not always known for her diplomatic skills, and her words, even at three, sent shivers down my spine. We cuddled together seeking what comfort each of us could provide. Little did I know at the time, but she was already heavily pregnant with my brother Leslie.

This family news could not have come at a worse time. The year was 1963 and it was Whitsuntide Bank Holiday Monday. We had only a few weeks earlier moved into 8 Park Place, having been nearly evicted from Bogs Lane. The house was not fully renovated and although a bathroom had just been installed, the wallpaper in the front room was in urgent need of replacement. Even worse, when it rained the roof leaked and water would flow down through the plaster ceiling, creating a number of puddles. Although several bowls were used for collecting the water, they weren't enough and water often hit the hard lino floor of the living room.

The fateful day in question was a Summer Bank Holiday and these – especially the rare hot ones – were always a busy time for my father's donkey business. This particular May Bank Holiday had been very hot and my father, in high expectations, had left home especially early. In addition to arranging to take his donkeys to the riverside, he had also agreed to assist at the Harrogate auction market which, despite the holiday, was still having a livestock sale. It was customary for his best friend Gerald Walker, a local butcher from Hookstone, Harrogate, to come along and assist. My father would introduce Gerald to visitors as the local strongman. Through regular flattery and encouragement by Dad and in support of their long-standing friendship, Gerald would be motivated to lift often very hefty children onto the donkeys all afternoon, for very little reward.

A darker side to this friendship was that Gerald was father's ideal drinking partner and could consume almost the same amount of beer, thus creating an almost perfect relationship, in so far as they were concerned.

By 1963, much of the work expected from Gerald had been delegated to younger men and boys, aptly known by everyone in the local area as the 'Donkey Boys'. This allowed both father and Gerald to engage in their first passion – heavy drinking. As I have alluded to at the start of this book, the place for this kind of activity was generally, but not exclusively, the George Hotel. Conveniently located near to the gateway leading to the riverside, the George provided the ideal venue for watching the donkeys from the beer garden in case of any trouble, and also the arrival of my mother, which (if father was caught in the pub) also meant trouble!

My earliest memory of being at this pub was sitting on one of its front patio seats drinking a bottle of lemonade. The George was a rather shabby affair with wooden floors and smoke-filled rooms. Like many pubs of its era it had known both good and bad times. Fittings from a more prosperous time, such as a room-call system and bits of expensive brassware, were still festooned behind the bar.

Licensing laws were different in those days and at around 3.30pm time had been called and Gerald and father found themselves standing at the entrance to Bilton Fields. Father said afterwards that he had had a premonition, and his whole life had flashed before him. Afterwards, very shaken, he told Gerald that he was going to die later that day – but Gerald in a typical bullish mood, told him he had drunk too much ale, and the matter was left at that. Certainly the day had not been without incident because earlier, Daisy, one of the donkeys, had kicked father very hard on his left knee.

Leaving the donkeys at the riverside, father decided to travel to the Harrogate livestock auction, which in those days was located off Skipton Road. Nearly every vehicle he had ever owned was dilapidated and his van on this occasion was no exception. Attempting to turn off Skipton Road, he misjudged the turning, yanked at the steering wheel and snapped it off. The van hit a nearby tree and came to a noisy and shuddering halt.

The impact of the collision caused father's left leg to hit the crude metal dashboard and break. Evidently, the wound was open and blood gushed out at speed.

One of the donkeys promotes a derby. In the
early days everyone had to help.

Quick thinking by other drivers resulted in the calling of an ambulance and the immediate provision of some elementary first aid.

Father was taken in a semi-conscious state to Harrogate General Hospital, where it appeared his chances of living were rated 50/50. A blood transfusion was completed and surgeons then worked during the night on his broken leg. Due to the severity of the injuries, the specialist decided to insert a stainless steel plate just below the knee. From all accounts this was completed without too much difficulty and father's broken bones were temporarily pinned together and afterwards he was taken on to a ward.

For the first twenty-four hours it was 'touch and go' as to whether he lived or died. He was later to comment that those nearest death were placed at the entrance to the ward, so in the event of dying they could be quickly removed without disturbing other patients. It was perhaps, then, to father's relief and that of the family that after a few days, he graduated from the doorway to the middle of the ward.

Life on the limbs ward for patient David Walter Allott was slow and tedious but, thankfully for all of us, recovery started virtually immediately and went almost without any notable events. In total he spent some six weeks recuperating, organising impromptu parties and generally undermining nursing rules along with those laid down by the management.

Father was a fanatical smoker, not in the volume he smoked, but at what particular times. Smoking on the hospital ward was generally allowed around meal times and in the evenings, along with what almost seemed like chain smoking when on the hospital's veranda.

He used to smoke 'Park Drive' tipped, which as a child I thought were connected to the street near to Park Place, but obviously in reality nothing could have been further from the truth.

Following father's requests, relatives took to smuggling cigarettes into the ward during visiting hours. In those days visiting was limited to an hour each afternoon and a further one each evening, so cigarettes were needed by many, and especially by father, just to fill up the day!

My recollection of events is incomplete, but I do remember that grandfather and grandmother promised to take me as soon as possible to visit him. As a child I eagerly looked forward to this visit and can recall some of it still quite vividly despite the massive passage of time.

My grandparents called to collect mother and me in their black Austin car. Mother was pregnant with my brother Leslie and, some weeks later, would be a patient herself at the same hospital. The journey from Park Place to the now closed Harrogate General Hospital, which was opposite a trailer park on Knaresborough Road, took only around ten minutes.

Young children were forbidden to go on the ward, so arrangements were made for me to be discreetly taken into the central courtyard, thereby avoiding the hospital's reception. The hospital was one of those old fashioned colonial-style complexes where nearly every ward had its own veranda, despite the UK's (then) generally inclement weather.

By prior arrangement, father was laying on his bed, which had been specially pulled out onto the balcony. His left leg was covered in a large white plaster cast, which was slung via a traction system high above the bed.

The male side of the Allott family was not renowned for expressing their emotional feelings and this visit typified the situation. Pleased to see father, I just sat there looking at him and the leg. Mother passed some reading material to him, a Dalesman and the Horse & Hound, along with the Yorkshire Post. Grandfather talked about the poor weather and his need to get in control of the garden, while grandmother had a parallel conversation with me about hospitals.

Despite the restricted visiting time of one hour, it seemed to drag on forever. At the end of visiting, which had by now reduced everyone to silence, he was courteously kissed by nearly all the family and left once again on his own.

Notwithstanding father's incapacity, his donkeys had been booked for a number of riding jobs and also some donkey derbies. Mother had never really been involved with the donkeys – after all, he didn't want her spying on his drinking habits or, even worse, seeing how little work he did. Mother's support had been limited to handling the correspondence, so when father fell ill she was at a loss.

To lead and manage the donkeys, father always had a gang of young lads (girls were not employed until the late 1960s), who were recruited from the nearby council estates. Many of the lads did not have a lot going for them and they were grateful for the money and sometimes the odd bit of parenting father imposed.

One of the exceptions to this rule was a tall young lad called David Shepherd. His father, Edgar, had become friendly with my own father and the two would chat for hours. Edgar had been the policeman in some nearby village, a career he later followed by taking a job first as a traffic warden and latterly as caretaker of a school for children with special needs. Father liked him and it wasn't long before Edgar, in between his other duties, started helping at peak times with the donkeys as he had earlier assisted my family with the renovation of Park Place, before we moved in.

Prior to father's injuries, little had been done in the way of business planning. What little consideration had been given by him to the future generally took place in the pub over a number of beers. But the friendship with the Shepherds turned out to be highly fortuitous at this difficult time and, within the space of a couple of days, Edgar had been summoned to the general hospital to receive his instructions.

By all accounts the Shepherds did a good job running the donkeys; bookings were completed on schedule and seemingly without hitch. However, while the Shepherds were practical, a number of items concerning animal behaviour had eluded them. The most important of these concerned a small stallion donkey, which father had purchased prior to breaking his leg. It had always been his ambition to breed donkeys and this small, aggressive donkey, bought from a dealer in Leeds, was there to help fulfil this ambition.

It is normal stock practice to keep male and female animals separated. For some reason, however, Edgar Shepherd decided to run the Jack (male) donkey with all the Jennies (females). When questioned about the wisdom of this move, Edgar had reassured my father by saying that the Jack had shown no interest in any of the others and was behaving well. Unfortunately for everyone, this was far from the truth. Within the space of a matter of months, the majority of the female donkeys had been made pregnant, which meant their foals would arrive the following summer (a donkey carries its foal for 12 months), right at the peak trading time. The relationship between Edgar and father deteriorated once the pregnancies were discovered, although in fairness to both they still used to meet up and talk.

Father spent his six weeks in hospital recuperating in reasonably high spirits before being unleashed on the world once again. He had always been a bit of a hypochondriac and the chance to draw attention to himself with crutches gave him the opportunity, which he milked to the last drop. Able-bodied people were encouraged to give way to him, those resisting were pushed or even thumped with a crutch. Mother's meal

This is an early picture of Gerald Walker and father after a few hours drinking.

timetable had to be adjusted to accommodate father's changing fancies, but best of all he could simply lie in bed all day on the basis of feeling ill.

However, despite his semi-incapacitation and indifference to others, I think he was genuinely pleased to have survived the crash and set about making the best of things. His first task was to visit his beloved donkeys and this was achieved on the day following his discharge from the hospital.

The journey to Bogs Lane and the adjacent grazing at the petrol dump was undertaken by me and father in a car belonging to one of his friends. The donkeys were all grazing at a rough five-acre site which had been used for the underground storage of petrol during the war.

For some reason, possibly to do with the Cold War, the Government had retained ownership of the site, but allowed the summer grazing rights to be let to my father on an annual basis. The main advantage was that the donkeys could spend the summer there; this allowed a hay crop, a vital part of the donkey food production programme, to be harvested from Mrs Todd's field at Bogs Lane. A further big plus was that the site was near enough to the Todd land to allow the donkeys to be walked down in a matter of minutes.

Father duly arrived on his bright yellow crutches and surveyed the site. The fact that more than half his herd of donkeys was pregnant did not escape him. Annoyance turned to anger and the air turned blue as father unleashed a volley of swearwords, which lasted for around ten minutes. One of his special skills was to be able to swear for at least fifteen minutes without repeating himself even once!

Frustrated and concerned, he returned to Park Place to contemplate the future. On the surface things didn't look too bright, his broken leg prevented chimney sweeping and his female donkeys were all expecting, a situation which would impact greatly on the following year's plans. In typical style, he went out into Knaresborough complete with crutches and set about drinking the town dry. On the occasions this happened father called it his bit of relaxation, but mother and I called it hell.

Space at Park Place was rather limited. Father tended to dominate the front room and the only other downstairs area was a large kitchen-cum-living room. Life at Park Place was often harsh as the house was full of draughts and lacked any form of central heating.

After a few weeks back from hospital, father started complaining about chest pains and this went on for a number of days, but it was brushed off by his doctor as indigestion. Whether his drinking and love of eating sometimes strange, fatty foods had anything to do with the prognosis, we shall never know. However, as part of his post-accident treatment, his doctor suggested that he should attend an out-patient clinic once a week and this was duly arranged.

It was customary with the NHS in those days to send an ambulance around to collect the patients. The ambulance arrived on the following Tuesday at around lunchtime. A member of the crew took one look at my father and then asked him if he felt ill. Father relayed his story about chest pains and he was then told not to move. Father was rushed into hospital and subsequently diagnosed by doctors as having a thrombosis. It was lodged in his leg, although for reasons I am uncertain about, affected other parts of his body.

His second hospitalisation was far more difficult than the first. Doctors advised mother that he could die and father was instructed to lie still. Blood-thinning medication was prescribed (better known as Warfarin, which is used in some rat poisons) and after around four weeks he was allowed home.

At about this time my mother was also admitted to hospital and on the 16th of July 1963, gave birth to my brother Leslie David. During this upheaval I was sent to the grandparents and looking back it seemed mighty odd to be visiting both of my parents in the same hospital!

As a young child I found life in 1963 particularly tough, as all attention was given to my brother and father, making me feel somewhat neglected. Father was generally in a grumpy mood, which added to my own gloom.

After this second hospitalisation my father became convinced that he was a cripple and no amount of discussion with his own father would convince him otherwise. From that time on, walking sticks would be used whenever he felt low or needed sympathy from the family.

His attitude took a marked change for the worse following the thrombosis. Often he would stay in bed until 11am. Looking back it would seem that he was obviously suffering from post-accident depression, although in those times the health service did not concern itself with such minor details!

Thereafter, he suffered various bouts of depression. During his lowest points, he would chastise me over very minor issues, often clipping me and generally being very grumpy. Part of the reason for his depression was the fact that following the accident, his chimney sweep business was finished and because of his health, cattle droving was, at least for now, out too. This resulted in less money coming into the household.

To compensate, he devoted the majority of his efforts towards his donkey business, enabling it at its peak to build up to a herd of twenty donkeys. During the winter of 1963 he had to rely on external help from Mapplebeck's 'cattle hauliers' who took charge of getting the donkeys out to their winter homes, usually with friendly, nearby farmers.

Not a great deal of any significance happened during the winter of 1963, with father spending most of the time feeling sorry for himself, which was bad news for everyone.

Chapter 5

Moving Forward

Father decided that his main income would have to be the donkeys and resources were allocated to ensure this was achieved. The New Year, however, started badly when the saddle room was broken into and a number of pieces of equipment were stolen. However, the police soon arrested a young man caught trying to sell the harness, and the matter came to court with a successful conviction in the February. Father was further annoyed when two donkeys, Muffin and Jenny, which had been lent for the winter to Arkendale Hall, a large estate based in the village of the same name, on the east of Knaresborough, were sent back early due to their unsuitability.

Purchasing of donkey equipment went on all the time and father bought a saddle for £2.50 during the first week of January. Father's 1964 diary indicates that preparations for the summer donkey season started in earnest at the beginning of March.

He made up a number of bell collars on the 2nd and started to do up the harness on the 3rd. On Thursday the 4th, he saw Jack Mapplebeck, owner of the cattle wagon business, to discuss the coming season and what jobs would require transport. Some of the donkey bookings he had were for riding jobs, which were better known as 'ball breakers' due to the heavy lifting involved.

At the top of the list of 'ball breakers' were the American Independence Day celebrations at Menwith Hill, a United States communications station to the west of Harrogate, just off Skipton Road. The donkeys were always popular with the (often hefty) children who lived in the family quarters and father used to nickname the base, the 'yank camp'.

Other jobs also appeared on the list. However, for some of them at least, he would have to take a back seat with regards to lifting the children onto the donkeys, because of the metal plate in his leg.

A list recovered from his diary records nine jobs in total comprising riding at Menwith Hill and Bintex (a latex foam factory later called Dunlopillo, near Harrogate), together with donkey derbies at Leeds, Keighley, Halifax, Ossett, Colne, Sowerby Bridge and Rawdon. The transport to get to these events was a cattle wagon and the cost of getting to each Yorkshire job, where all the derbies took place, except Colne which is over the Yorkshire border in Lancashire, was around £9, all negotiated in advance.

The little foal was called Jack and was given to the author

Father's diary records that his average charge for a donkey derby was £35, with this money coming into the household in addition to the donkey riding cash generated from the riverside undertaking.

Although the cattle wagon haulage business was owned by Jack Mapplebeck, various drivers were involved in taking the donkeys to jobs. These included his brother Maurice and Ken Mothersill, a nice but outspoken northerner, who lived on the Harrogate Broadacres council estate and whose sons Kevin (briefly) and Norman (for a long time) were also donkey boys.

My own favourite driver was Maurice, although it would not be until I was five that I would travel with him. Maurice, who was a family friend as well as a provider of transport, always covered for my father when he had drunk to excess. His parents also lived on Bogs Lane, and ran a coal business and smallholding for many years. These connections ran very deep and father would sometimes hire from them the small paddock next to Mrs Mapplebeck's bungalow, when one of his donkeys was in foal.

Maurice was one of those kindly people who, as I got older, would try to protect me from father's rages. In later years he would try teaching me some diplomacy in order to avoid unnecessary conflicts. As a former Second World War junior army officer, he also had his health problems, arising from an injured back received when a trainee tank crew took him over a cliff edge. Therefore, where donkey-riding jobs were involved, father would normally have at least one strongman to accompany him to a job, or as he would call them, the heavy mob.

The saddles used on the donkeys were stored at Park Place for the winter and Gerald Walker kindly agreed on the Thursday to take them up to Bogs Lane. In preparation, father had a number of new saddle handles drilled at Henry's, the ironmongers. At this time of year he would work particularly hard, driven on by the expectation of a bumper summer. Key activities included arranging the silver plating of donkey bells, painting of donkey boards and the preparation of the actual donkeys.

At Easter, it was his strategy to have just a handful of donkeys at home in order to keep his business costs down. George Collier, the local black-smith, had dutifully come on the Wednesday prior to the holiday week-end and cut Muffin, Mary, Jenny and Judy's hooves. Punch apparently was fine. In anticipated excitement of a good Bank Holiday, father took the seat for the donkey helpers to rest on and the donkey tying posts down to the riverside on the Thursday afternoon.

Good Friday was always the official start date, and in eager excite-ment father was up at 10.30am. After eating his usual breakfast diet of bacon and eggs, he would already be coughing and spluttering with nervous stress. His chosen work attire for donkey riding or racing was a yellow smock, light tan horse-dealer's boots, an open-necked shirt and a pair of fawn or brown cord trousers. On important days such as Bank Holidays father could be physically sick in the street, in anticipation of the demanding day ahead.

Within thirty minutes of getting up, he would have finished reading the Yorkshire Post, climbed into his van and travelled off – usually with the driver's side door open – to the Bogs Lane site, which was a few miles away.

At 1pm two donkey lads would arrive at Bogs Lane and three donkeys would be saddled up and walked down to the Knaresborough riverside. Father's diary records: "Came on fine following rain, took 10 shillings (50 pence)!" Such a disappointing start must have played badly on my father who would be now in debt, after all the preparation costs.

The Saturday was a write-off with cold weather and rain. It would seem that the Sunday was not much better and takings were just 17s 6d (17 shillings and sixpence), i.e. less than £1.00. On the Bank Holiday Monday he took £2.50 and then it was very cold until the following Sunday, when things took a decided turn for the better and father took a much-improved £40.00.

Father's life muddled along from one day to the next, often inter-spersed with bouts of binge drinking at various well-known hostelries. Meanwhile the remaining donkeys slowly arrived home from their winter lodgings for the summer season, many of them now heavily in foal.

On the Thursday, father's loyal cattle driving and guard dog, Roy, was run over by a car. Roy's eyesight had been failing for the last couple of years and over the previous few months it had virtually gone. Father was naturally very upset and buried him under a tree at Bogs Lane, with a promise that he would be reburied if the field was ever vacated.

One of the highlights of the year was the arrival (after twelve months) of the various foals. Given that the pregnant donkeys had not been able to take part in the season's earlier donkey

Father insisted that when family visitors were around their children all got a free donkey ride. In this picture the author is giving his cousin, David Gill a ride on Sammy, whilst the baby's mother Margaret Knight née Allott, holds him firmly to the saddle. The look of disinterest on the young author's face says it all.

derbies, father was somewhat relieved when the animals started giving birth. The majority of these arrivals took place in July and it would seem from the business records that some of these births were difficult; it therefore must have been quite a traumatic period.

Jenny was unable to deliver her foal. Clearly in pain, she walked up to father for help. It seems that despite his gruffness the donkeys knew that if they were in difficulties (feeling ill, having pregnancy troubles, or whatever) he would sort them out. With his assistance the foal was carefully manipulated out and within a few minutes was standing up suckling its first lot of milk. The foal was a lovely white colour with a distinctive black cross along its back (most donkeys have a black cross on their backs, which is said to have been given to all of them after Jesus rode one on Palm Sunday) and was given the name Rosy. The following year, this young donkey was given to my (baby) sister Katherine as a pet. A few days afterwards, more foals were born. The next two were called Jack and Jill.

Jack was a cute black donkey and Jill was a light grey colour. Their mothers both proudly fawned over them and pushed or kicked away any of the other donkeys that came up to take a look and got too close. Jack was given to me as a pet and Jill to Leslie. The arrival of the foals thankfully lifted father's still gloomy mood.

The fourth donkey to have a foal was Mary, a dark multi-coloured donkey who had a blue and white coat. Immediately after delivering her foal she started attacking it. Firstly she tried to bite it and then attempted to kick it. Father feared for the foal's life and had to separate them. He tried various techniques in an effort to get the mother to accept the new foal, but all without any success. This posed a major problem for father because without milk from its mother the foal would soon die. One extreme option was to have a vet put the foal down. However, he felt this would be a needless waste of a young animal's life.

After a bit of quick thinking, father phoned the Kirbys, a farming family who lived at Bishop Thornton, which is a rural village a few miles from Harrogate on the way to Pateley Bridge. George Kirby had provided a winter home for a donkey for a few years for his daughter Linda to ride. Father explained his dilemma and, for reasons I am still not clear about, Linda agreed to rear the foal by bottle-feeding it. Perhaps not surprisingly, as the foal grew up, it thought Linda was its mother and brayed and shouted whenever she went into the field. The foal was given by father to the Kirbys and was subsequently named Sammy by them. It was never reunited with its hostile mother or the rest of the donkeys and lived its life with the Kirbys at their farm until it died of old age.

Within a few weeks the foals could be left together for a few hours, enabling their proud mothers to go to the riverside to give rides. But it would be many months before they could stay on their own long enough for father to take their mothers off donkey racing.

Chapter 6

Getting More Donkeys

In May 1964, there were two pressing problems. The first was transport, as the original van had been written off in the accident the previous year and the second was the urgent need for more racing donkeys.

After scouring the Harrogate Advertiser for a number of weeks, father spotted a large van for sale in Starbeck at the Claro Laundry Company. I went with him to see it and the manager of the laundry, a rather generous man who indulged me with sweets, soon became putty in my father's hands and fell easy prey to his patter. "What's the least you will take?" asked my father rather aggressively. After a bit of a negotiating tussle which father easily won, a deal was struck for £10. When we came to drive the van away, the manger was somewhat taken aback after father retrieved two crutches from outside his office door. His driving was at the best of times risky, but with his left leg very stiff it was a nightmare. As a young lad I was, of course, still largely oblivious to the dangers involved.

As soon as father had spent a number of days painting the van to remove the former owner's lettering, he went off to the Building Society and withdrew a wad of notes. It was then time to go off to Leeds to talk with 'PC99', better known as Harry Taylor. Not a lot was happening in Knaresborough so we all set off together, as a trip to Leeds was the highlight of our week.

Harry earned his nickname from impersonating a police officer in order to confiscate items that had been stolen in an earlier burglary. He was a very tall, well-built man, who had large sideburns. He always told a good story and was one of those streetwise dealers who had the connections to buy almost anything a horse dealing business, or in fact any business, might need.

Harry's connections extended to donkeys and a whole network of gypsies who often owned them. Many of these people lived on streets that had been bombed out in World War Two and were awaiting redevelopment. In the early 1960s it was quite common to see an assortment of horses, goats, donkeys and ponies tethered on such semi-neglected sites.

However, mere details such as where the donkeys originally lived did not matter a jot to my father. His main concern was to obtain more donkeys and fulfil his desire to take at least twelve animals racing, which

This picture was taken around 1963/4. Mrs Olga Nelson gives her son David a donkey ride. The young boys sitting on the bench were the donkey leaders (known as the donkey boys).

was not currently possible as most of his mares were looking after their recently delivered foals.

Harry was a good friend to my father and over the coming years this exercise would be repeated many times, mostly whilst I was in attendance, hence my background knowledge.

On arrival at Harry's terraced property on the northern edge of Leeds city centre, father consumed two or three large whiskies over a great deal of banter. After negotiating a commission, Harry then picked up the phone and talked to the travellers who had telephones. As for the rest, Harry ringed their house or camp locations with a pen on an old ripped map for a subsequent visit.

Father also had a long-term hiring arrangement with a Leeds family called Kindon and occasionally from a successful but tough-talking horse dealer called Warren. Dealing with these families was stressful, but they were useful fall-back suppliers. It was the sellers' custom in those days to liberally dispense whisky and beer to any potential buyer in order to soften them up and father's receipt of hospitality on this particular visit was no different.

After a number of quick trips around nearby potential dealers which had earlier been suggested by Harry, and a subsequent visit to Mrs Kindon, four donkeys were purchased and another two hired for the

York race course around July 1967. The young child in the pram is Paul who is now also, like his father, a bookmaker.

coming season. Two of these donkeys were then rammed in the back of father's van and we subsequently set off back home.

Father had a pretty vicious temper after a few drinks and his personality could switch from jovial to angry in the time it takes to flip a coin. Inebriated and also tired from his escapades with Harry, he just wanted to get home and sleep. Mother and I instinctively kept quiet on the way back in the van knowing that with father it would not take much for matters to get out of hand. On our arrival at Bogs Lane, the two donkeys were unceremoniously booted out and he then drove down to Knaresborough, enabling me to retire to bed.

By mid-1964, the donkey business was really starting to take off. There seemed to be a number of reasons for this, not least being father's decision to levy a price increase for derbies.

Amazingly, on the riding side of the business, he charged sixpence (2½ pence current money) a ride from the 1950s right through to the 1970s and still managed to make some kind of limited living. For example, on the 17th May 1964 – a Bank Holiday Sunday – the diary reported that the business took £24, not bad for an afternoon's wages, when many people did not earn that for a week's work. Wages for Colin and Norman, the young lads who helped with the donkeys are recorded at five shillings each. The Whit Monday was marred by rain but father still managed to make £15. On the Tuesday he made £12 and gave Fred

Hawkes, his very loyal elderly helper, £1. His business logic was very simple – four donkey rides equalled a pint of beer. This is a far cry from today, where in Cleethorpes and Blackpool, one donkey ride now costs more than a single pint!

A great deal of 'to-ing and fro-ing' of donkeys took place in the early and mid 1960s, and it generally involved the Warrens and Kindons. As time progressed father was determined to break the hold that these two families held over his business, and by the late 1960s they were no longer supplying any of his donkeys.

Chapter 7

The Business

August was traditionally a good month for the donkeys, with reasonable takings generated from the day-trippers. August 1964 was, however, very disappointing and between the 6th and the 20th it seemed to rain almost every day, causing havoc to the business.

Father also suffered pain and depression following his broken leg and thrombosis. On many of the August mornings his breakfast, always consisting of bacon and eggs, turned to rubber under the grill while waiting for him to surface. On some mornings he never got up before 12 o' clock which, looking back, must have placed a strain on our poor, long-suffering mother. The diary for August records takings of little more than £1 on most of the weekdays. Outgoings were on-going and the diary records that Warren got £20 and Mrs Kindon £6 for two jobs. Only the donkey derbies were providing a regular income to sustain the business.

By mid-September father was despatching his donkeys out to the many farmers who provided winter homes for them. By the middle of the

Local jockeys were hired at this fund-raising event to lead the donkeys.

The donkeys also attended countless little jobs. Two donkeys and boys attended a private event in Knaresborough

following month nearly all had been lent out and he was moving towards his winter chores.

At this time in his life, the onset of winter also included lots of moaning and groaning and late starts. Various transactions are recorded for the month of October, notably the purchase of hay and harness, including three donkey bells from the horse fair at Yarm.

A number of entries in the 1964 diary are recorded as 'sick days' and also show that one of father's key helpers in the early days, Fred Hawks, died. Over the years, in fits and starts, Fred had played a big part in helping father to get started with his donkeys.

The end of the year was the time for hedging and harness repairs in preparation for the new season.

However, during the winter of 1964 father's left leg, which was now reinforced with a steel plate due to his earlier accident, started to cause him considerable pain. Part of the problem was cold weather, which caused the plate to contract, which then nipped up his leg and hurt when he walked.

Father loved the horse fairs and would often get very drunk with his many gypsy friends. At that time there were many of the old gypsy fairs still on the go including Barnaby (Boroughbridge), Topcliffe, Appleby, Lee Gap and, of course, Yarm. This latter fair was the highlight of the year and where possible father would stay overnight (see chapter 15). Yarm fair was ideal for getting drunk with the local gypsies and he looked forward to it every year. The diary records that father stayed for a few days and returned home on the 20th October. I enjoyed his return because he always brought back a small present and on this occasion it was a red Dinky-toy dumper truck.

By November 1964, father's winter plans were already unravelling with various donkeys being sent home by some of the host farmers. These included Muffin, Tiny, Sammy and Mary. Each donkey at home for the winter was another mouth to feed, which meant less money for our family because of the need to purchase extra hay to supplement the crop father grew.

Chapter 8

The Death of Leslie

In late November my little brother Leslie contracted meningitis. He was a blue-eyed, blond boy who enjoyed copying everything I did and sometimes, despite his young age, he would play shops with me. Dr Robinson, who was the family doctor at that time, was called to the house and after examining Leslie he had a lengthy discussion with my parents about my brother's illness, which at this stage he had failed to properly diagnose.

It was agreed that his cot would be placed downstairs near the all-night coal fire, as this was the warmest place in the house, and the doctor then started to call almost daily. By early December Leslie's condition had grown worse and I still vividly remember the doctor panicking and calling an ambulance early one Saturday evening to take Leslie and father to the hospital. Sadly, Leslie died during the night, just nineteen months old. We were all very shocked by his sudden death and a gloom settled over the house, which lasted on and off until the following summer.

The funeral arrangements were horrible and my father wore his dark suit and black shoes, which only saw the light of day for christenings, weddings and, of course, funerals. Leslie was buried in the section reserved in the Knaresborough cemetery for children and afterwards we all returned to Park Place for ham sandwiches and tea. It was a very low-key affair, as both my parents were devastated by the death of their youngest son.

For many months my parents were extra protective towards me and when I started school on a regular basis later in December, father would come down to collect me, often at least twenty minutes before the end of the school day.

The doom and gloom over the household lifted when my mother, who was heavily pregnant with my sister Katherine, went into labour prematurely on December the 23rd, the day after my own birthday.

Father had no idea how to look after himself, let alone other people. He woke me on the 23rd to say that mother had been taken into hospital because a stork was delivering my sister. He then set about preparing my breakfast. As a young boy of just five my normal breakfast was cereal. Father, bless him, insisted on cooking me a hearty bacon and eggs in the frying pan because this was his own normal breakfast. After this, a small

Family donkey riding: David gives his two children, Leslie (left) and Philip (right) a free donkey
ride at the riverside on Alice and Muffin, 1964.

suitcase was packed and I was taken to stay yet again with my grandparents at Moorland View, Starbeck.

That Christmas was jolly at Grandfather Allott's and I was allowed to get up to all kinds of mischief, which included parading around in my policeman's uniform, brought to me courtesy of Father Christmas. But the highlight of Christmas Day was the return of my mother on a stretcher to Morland View, with Katherine, just before lunch.

January 1965 set off slowly – it was a cold winter and a depression still hung over the family household. The winter Saturdays would follow a very consistent pattern; father would get up at around 10 o' clock, have breakfast and then the pair of us would travel in his van, to Bogs Lane in order to feed the donkeys and cut up logs with an axe or small bushman saw for the weekend.

After feeding the donkeys, we would spend around a couple of hours cutting up the logs to take home for the fire. At the age of just five, my task was to try and hold the wood still, whilst father cut it.

Later on a Saturday, around teatime, Gerald Walker would arrive. For more than thirty years Gerald always brought my family a free joint of meat for Sunday lunch. His kindness and friendship to father lasted his lifetime.

In the mid-1960s, domestic life in the Allott household during winter was very humdrum and frankly boring. Saturday tea often consisted of sausages, beans and chips. On Sunday a light breakfast would be followed by feeding the donkeys and eating the meat that Gerald had kindly donated on the Saturday.

We nearly always had boiled eggs for Sunday tea. Entertainment was provided via the small black and white television that received BBC1 and later ITV, thanks to a small converter box given to us by a family friend, called Jim Taylor whose daytime occupation was that of an electrical engineer, which meant that at least we were provided with a channel choice.

As the reader will see from some of my later chapters many of the funnier events happened when father had been drinking. But between late October and March each year, apart from Christmas, father stopped drinking and always went 'tee-total.' This gave his body a chance to recuperate and recover from the heavy drinking sessions he had enjoyed – or suffered – in the summer.

Father would try to 'escape' during the winter by reading his books. It was ironic that despite his gruffness and often-unkempt appearance, he had one of the largest (and scruffiest) collections of the classics in Knaresborough.

Chapter 9

Racing in Harrogate

At the age of five I was only allowed to go to the odd local donkey derby and I still recall those occasions with some excitement. One derby was taking place in Harrogate and because it was early in the donkey season, the animals were still being grazed at Bogs Lane. Maurice the driver wore a back brace because of his earlier injuries. He was older than father and had a special knack of calming him down, whether he was drunk or sober.

Typically late, Maurice arrived in a very elderly cattle wagon, which stank in the main rear body area of pigs, despite being washed out with a hosepipe and given a large covering of sawdust. In later life Maurice reminded me of Corporal Jones in Dad's Army, due to his inclination to panic attacks. Father also suffered from stress attacks but amusingly – and repeatedly – instructed us all (the donkey lads) not to get Maurice into a panic.

The racing tack consisted of bridles, pads, tie-round numbers for each donkey, sheets and a large spare piece of rope (for emergency fence repairs). All was placed on the canopy over and above the cattle wagon's cab. The young helpers, lads aged between 11 and 15, would load the tack and lead in each donkey. After all the animals were in place, the lads had to clamber over them to reach the semi-safety of the overhead canopy.

I was protected from the rear of the cattle wagon during my early days with the donkeys, and was allowed to ride in the front. The cattle wagon had a top speed of around fifty miles per hour, although the speedometer read much lower due to a fault. I was expected to sit on the engine cover (which got very hot) in the middle of the cab while father occupied all of the passenger section of the seat because of his bad leg!

This was my introduction to donkey racing which was the family's main source of income. But for me as a young boy, the most exciting was not the racing but riding in the big cattle wagon for the first time.

As I got older father expected me to pull my weight at these events and it wasn't long before he also expected me to ride when requested, in order to win the beloved trophies and wretched silver cups back for the organisers, or to please some old buffer he had just met – and to whom he had promised a winner.

Many of the derbies were run by enthusiastic but not always very

By the mid-1960s the majority of riders were lads – note the formal racing gear.

gifted people, and father would go into his 'very important' mode and boss them all around. One such event in Harrogate had been organised by the rugby union football club to raise much-needed funds for the autumn. It was an annual event and although I have been unable to find the 1965 race card, I have located the one for the following year. The cost of attending for punters was two shillings (10p), with all proceeds going towards the club's playing and social amenities, according to the race programme.

My personal recollections are limited because one donkey derby blurs into another, and I attended a large number of them as a got older. But the format was nearly always the same. Seven or sometimes eight races would be held. Seven or eight donkeys would run in each race, with often an all-winners race at the end. Each race had a title – for example at the 1966 rugby club event the second race was called the Granby Gallop after an area close to the rugby ground.

People bought ownership of a donkey for each race and were allowed to call the animal a particular name, often to give publicity to a business

Julie Felix – Rothwell Park, Leeds June 1970: Julie was the guest attraction at a donkey derby organised by Rothwell and District Round Table at Rothwell Park near Leeds. At this event the author was required to hold the donkey whilst she had her picture taken to promote the event. In the 1960s Julie Felix was prominent on Britain's folk scene and she became the first artist of the genre to be signed up by a major record company (Delta). In 1968, she had her own TV series.

or organisation. Some of the more interesting names in the programme include 'Blackburn & Swallow', 'Topscreen out of High Harrogate', 'Mr TB Ledgeway' and 'Beer by Watney out of Red Barrel'.

On arrival the donkeys would be put into a makeshift pen and a number of them would be selected to race a few minutes after the bookies or tote had finished taking bets. Children from a local riding school would normally act as jockeys although in extreme cases I have seen organisers grabbing children out of the crowd to ride!

Money was raised between races from a variety of on-field ideas, including entertainment and refreshment stalls, raffle tickets and, of course, the beer tent – which brings me to the unofficial format of any donkey derby father was a party to. This decreed that he should go off to the beer tent as soon as he could make good his escape. Often he would not be seen again for many hours and when he did materialise he was generally well lubricated with beer or as the family usually put it 'well popped up.'

The event at the rugby club finished at around 5.15pm, soon after the

Racing in the late 1960s. Note the scruffy turnout of the riders, the only thing that was
compulsory was a riding hat.

last race, and after a quick unbridling of the donkeys, they were herded
into the cattle wagon after which its large steel door was firmly shut.
Most of the work was organised by Maurice and completed by the
donkey lads; father's main task at the end of each derby was to remain
sufficiently sober to collect the money, which was nearly always strictly
cash!

From around this time onwards I was allowed to travel to local riding
events and to take part in the odd derby providing I was under supervision. Later I was even given permission to lead one or more tamer
donkeys along Bilton Fields. To get to Bilton Fields required mother to
put me on a bus at Knaresborough bus station. Then at the Dropping
Well bus stop, father would ensure that the donkey boy assigned to help
me would be waiting patiently for the bus to arrive, to escort me down to
the donkeys. However, within a few years I would not only be leading the
donkeys, but also collecting the money.

Chapter 10

The Allott Family

Although this book is intended to be predominately about our father, it would be remiss of me if I did not give readers some background family information in order to help set a few things in context.

By the summer of 1966 mother was again heavily pregnant and almost without warning she was called into hospital because of her high blood pressure. To assist the family our Great Auntie Olga Kirk came to stay for a few days before Katherine and myself were banished to Pontefract to stay with the Kirks for the summer. Uncle Edwin was involved in electrical retailing and, according to father, invented the first car indicator system, 'a set of illuminated lights for turning corners' – because he was tired of getting his hand wet when it rained! As well as Uncle Edwin and Auntie Olga the Kirk household also included their daughter Moira. Unlike my parents they were incredibly well organised and at weekends even had time to entertain us. This included digging a hole 'to Australia', wine making and taking us to feed the swans close to the power station at nearby Ferrybridge.

On June the 29th 1966 my brother Raymond was born and the family, according to father, was complete. His logic went like this. Philip would be fed up with the donkeys (correct), Katherine would train as a teacher (correct) and younger brother Raymond would take over the business and do everything his father asked of him without question (not correct!).

During late August 1966, Katherine and I returned home and things in the Allott household slowly started to return to normal. However, much to my mother's annoyance, Selby John, a worker who had been engaged to lift children onto the donkeys, and who would later operate the roundabout, started turning up for lunch. It would seem he was encouraged to call by father, because he felt sorry for him. How Selby managed to eat two boiled eggs plus buttered bread while Raymond had his soiled nappies changed, often directly in front of him, I shudder to think!

In the November of that year my parents were starting to run out of money. A bank overdraft at the Midland Bank (now the HSBC) was at its maximum and no money was being generated. Father thought rather naively that he could just apply for dole money. Father was therefore somewhat taken aback when he was told at the local Labour Exchange office that because he was self-employed, he did not qualify for any unemployment benefits.

Ultimately, this resulted in a visit by Social Services in order to assess the family's needs. Money must have been incredibly tight because father stopped smoking for a whole week. Two hard-faced men visited the house, each carrying a large briefcase. Various embarrassing questions were asked of our parents. At one stage I remember mother saying: "We have a tin of soup left for lunch and then I am not sure what we will do." Father offered them the option of inspecting the cupboard, but not surprisingly they declined. After various bits of form filling, it was agreed that our parents would be given emergency social security money until further notice. Money was paid to my parents until spring the following year. Father said it cost £20 a week to run the household, which he seemed to think was a lot! This must have been one of the most humiliating experiences our proud parents can ever have experienced. Although I was still very young, this visit is still ingrained in my mind and is something I would never wish to witness or experience ever again.

When not helping with the donkeys my sister, brother and I attended Manor Road Infants School followed by Castle Yard Junior School and finally King James' School, all in Knaresborough. I found school particularly hard and would be teased incessantly about the donkeys. "See you're playing football today Allott, have you brought a spare pair of hooves?" asked one of my so-called school friends. Kids who father had sacked for incompetence would also pester me and make snide remarks.

Worst of all, some kids and their parents thought we might be gypsies on account of the donkey-keeping and they would go on incessantly about the mess gypsies made.

Castle Yard Junior was a Church of England School which was located near the castle and next to the police station, and I was there from the age of eight. Later my sister and brother were also sent there. The head at that time was Harry Colley, a tough headmaster who pulled lads around by their hair. Girls and boys were segregated and the girls had their own school at the other side of the castle yard car park, which also doubled up during school hours as a playground.

Both Castle schools had very limited facilities and for the boys the daily school assembly had to take place in the Old Town Hall in Knaresborough Market Place. School assemblies always had prayers and hymns and there was a formal hymn practice for thirty minutes on a Tuesday morning. Mr Colley doubled up as the local choirmaster at St John's Parish Church and the best lads would be streamed off to sing in his choir.

One of the most embarrassing incidents that took place was when father applied to be the Castle Yard School caretaker. Three people

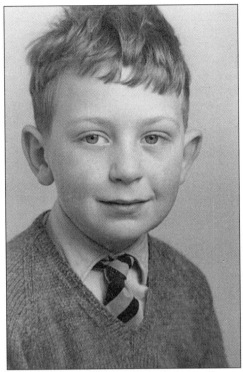

The author aged 7 in his Castle School uniform

applied for the job and sadly his application was not successful. When asked about working with children, father gave the headmaster a very patronising answer about how he earned a living from providing kids with entertainment. This highlighted to Mr Colley that his heart and soul might not be put into stoking the school boiler. After father's interview Mr Colley proceeded to call me David Allott for the remainder of my time at the school, despite my repeated protests!

It might be hard to imagine from what I have written so far about father, but he was a committed Christian who said the Lord's Prayer each evening. My parents therefore liked the idea of us going to a church school and did everything possible to encourage us to participate. During the winter Katherine regularly attended Sunday school and for a brief time so did Raymond.

Some of the teachers at Castle Yard School were already known by my parents. One of my teachers was Mrs Diana Smith, who many years later with her husband John would become one of my close friends. Other teachers included Mr Hopkinson, a music buff, and Mr Crispin, a former member of the RAF, who would dazzle the class with his wartime exploits.

School was stressful for all three of the Allott children because we knew that when lessons ended, father would have a nice lot of jobs lined up for us. During the summer these jobs would be exclusively concerned with the donkeys, but in winter it could mean anything from emptying ashes and laying the domestic fires, to doing the washing-up. Later in the 1970s when mother got a full-time job we were expected to peel potatoes and cook dinner in preparation for her arrival home.

None of us minded pulling our weight at home, but what we did find stressful was the fact that father would often sit in the house all afternoon and do nothing, and then order us all about and shout at us if we made the slightest mistake.

During the late 1960s life was still reasonably stress-free and we all came home from school for lunch each day. In August 1969 Grandmother Allott died suddenly of a heart attack whilst on a visit to Bath to see her daughter Margaret. She had been a diabetic for a number of years and the stress of the travelling along with over exertion caused by decorating a ceiling some three weeks earlier, was all too much for her heart. Thereafter Grandfather Allott started coming for his lunch on school days and this lasted until his second marriage to Mary Walker in June 1970.

Grandfather, like father, was an impatient type and after I kept everyone waiting for fifteen minutes for lunch one day, I got questioned. The problem was quickly identified as another school lad who was chasing me around Knaresborough on my way home. Father thought that the lad was doing a really good job as it meant I always got home promptly for lunch, but Grandfather was less pleased because of the potential bullying. A two-pronged approach was devised to solve the matter; grandfather would wait in a shop doorway and club the lad with his walking stick and father would give me some fighting lessons to beat him up. Fortunately, grandfather never had to club the lad but I did shortly afterwards give him a good hiding and thereafter the Allott lunchtimes passed with little or no incident.

In September 1971 I attended King James, the former local grammar school. This required a more formal school uniform, so the home-made grey pullovers and trousers I had worn for Castle were a non-starter. King James' uniforms were generally purchased by mother from a local store on the High Street, using a Government grant given on account of our limited family income. Kids wearing the subsidised uniforms could easily be identified on account of the cheap grey trousers and blazer, as I discovered on my first day.

King James' School organised a fund-raising gala day each year during the summer. Teachers would run stalls and other entertainment, with the money raised going into school funds. The head teacher decided that father should be invited, along with his donkeys, to give rides. The summer Saturday chosen for the event was full of intermittent rain. Drizzling rain is one of the worst things in the donkey trade because while it is generally not raining enough to cease work, it can be sufficiently bad to damage the harness. This caused father to get into a temper and, after setting the donkeys up on the school playing fields, he retreated to the nearby Marquis of Granby pub to drown his sorrows.

Returning to the school field about an hour later, tanked up on four pints of beer, father was not in the mood to be trifled with. At about this point my metalwork teacher, who spoke with a lisp, came over to complain. "Excuse me Mr Allott but could you move your donkeys elsewhere as they are walking over my putting holes and also filling them all with manure!" spluttered the somewhat self-righteous teacher.

"I tell you what I will do, old cock, I will take the wretched things all home," responded father, very aggressively.

Now extremely embarrassed, I rather boldly said "You should not speak to my teacher this way, it's a bit rude." Father, snarling, said: "I am not going to be told what to do by some jumped-up little school teacher who talks as though he has a sock stuffed down his throat, whatever you might think."

The teacher stood there expressionless. He was clearly not used to being spoken to in this way. Meantime, I rolled my eyes while the teacher remained speechless and looked at the ground. This was not really surprising, given the fact that he had been publicly humiliated in front of one of his own pupils! Needless to say my school metalwork exam and end of term report were not very good that year.

Father never really learnt from his mistakes and he had a real knack sometimes for mucking things up simply because he flew off the handle at the least provocation.

As touched on elsewhere in this book, in winter the donkeys always had to be fed each day and sometimes twice a day if the weather was really bad. To break the monotony of this, father always liked someone from the family to help him. On this particular Saturday Katherine, who was at the time aged around 13, had drawn the short straw and the pair set off in father's van to attend to the donkeys.

Father was always defensive at the best of times and people blocking his access or worse parking in the lane at Harrogate Road would nearly always be seen as some kind of threat. Arriving at the field, father was dismayed to find a car blocking the entrance to the lane, which clearly made it impossible for him to go up it. He was furious and started swearing and twittering about how it was a "bloody cheek" and that the occupant should get it shifted forthwith!

On occasions like this father would make Katherine stay in the van to protect her from any abusive language. The fact that he nearly always generated most of it did not seem to register with him! He was very rude to the driver who had unavoidably broken down and was now waiting for an accident truck to collect him. The troubled motorist turned out to be the curate from St John's, who Katherine knew from Sunday school and her confirmation classes.

The curate thought, because he knew Katherine and her Christian values, it wouldn't be a problem sorting his car out in the lane, pending further help. Unfortunately, father had wound himself up so much he didn't realise who he was talking to and even when it was pointed out to him by the poor frightened curate that father was speaking to a man of the church, it simply inflamed the situation. Father said "I don't care if you're Jesus Himself; you're not leaving your car here while it gets mended! Get the bloody thing shifted now!"

When father got back in the car he complained to Katherine that the bloke in the lane had been pretending to be a vicar, but that it hadn't fooled him! Katherine of course realised who it was and told father in a somewhat exasperated voice who the man was. "Well," said father, "He won't park there again!".

The next time Katherine saw the poor curate she had to apologise, because by the end of the argument he had seen her sitting in the van and hadn't understood why she had not got out to defend him. The whole episode was extremely embarrassing; the curate never fully forgave Katherine and thereafter tried to avoid her.

Chapter 11

Holidays

Unlike most families, it was not possible for us to take holidays during the summer because of the donkey riding, and therefore we were restricted to taking a break at the end of the season – money permitting of course.

Father would only go to one destination for his holiday and that was Whitby. From 1969 onwards, the family took a week's annual break in mid or late September. If the chosen departure day was a warm Sunday, father would first work the donkeys by the riverside with our help and then use the money raised to help fund the holiday spending money.

As a result of working often until 6pm, the journey to Whitby would start early evening which meant that by the time we were halfway to the east coast it would already be dark. Father was never very good at map reading and could on occasions even get lost in Harrogate! This often meant it could take anything up to three hours for us to reach our destination, compared to just an hour and a half nowadays.

Our normal mode of travel to Whitby was in one of father's vans which, as far as the Bedfords or subsequent Ford Transits were concerned, required the fitting of an extra seat in the rear. We used a bus seat, which had been bought from a Starbeck scrap yard.

The vans were not normally used for long distances as their regular journeys consisted of little more than travelling the two miles to the Harrogate Road fields and back. Longer journeys revealed any weakness in the vehicles and this resulted in a number of near disasters: a petrol pump hose unclipping and squirting fuel all over the passenger in the front seat, burned-out clutches and faulty oil seals on the engine drain plug. On at least two occasions things going awry with a van required the calling out of a recovery vehicle to help us, even though we had managed to complete most of the journey and were on the edge of Whitby!

One of the reasons father liked going to Whitby was because the town, which is at the edge of the North Yorkshire Moors on one side and the North Yorkshire Moors on the other, is very similar to Knaresborough. Both towns have a history dating back to medieval times and both are controlled by a nearby borough council which, in the case of Whitby, is Scarborough.

Whitby is a close-knit community and many of the older families have fishing roots in the community that date back hundreds of years.

Philip, Katherine and Raymond dig in the sand at Whitby aided by the dog Jill

Historically, the town was an important fishing port and it was where Captain James Cook took his seaman's apprenticeship before subsequently sailing the 'Endeavour' from Whitby harbour.

Tom Dawson, a former farm hand would look after the donkeys while father was away and, if necessary, provide them with daily hay. One animal, however, always travelled with the Allotts and this was the family's pet dog called Jill. She had been bought by father in the mid-1960s and her primary purpose in life was to retrieve the game when father was shooting. On holiday Jill would sleep in the back of the van and the rest of us would be in self-catering accommodation, usually on the West Cliff area. This was booked by mother, based on price, in order to meet the family's basic requirements.

Most families go on holiday to do various things together and this was not much different with the Allotts. At lunchtimes, however, father would go drinking with the Fortunes – the famous Whitby kipper curers from whom, as mentioned in chapter one, he learnt the donkey trade. He enjoyed nothing more than discussing old times and his friendship with the Fortunes also allowed him to mix socially with many of the fishing people. The lunchtime drinking sessions could last for a few hours, after which father would emerge red-faced and try to participate in some family game or other.

My parents had no understanding of the effects of the sun and therefore no-one in the family was protected with suntan cream. When the weather was hot, all three children turned bright red in the early part of the holiday, so perhaps it was lucky that we did not go in high season!

Entertainment in the evenings was limited to television, walks and fishing in the harbour under the Whitby swing bridge. During these sessions father would talk about Whitby, the Fortunes and those who subsequently took over the local donkey business. One of the stories he told that I can still vividly remember concerned the seaside donkeys: during the early days of the Whitby donkeys it was common practice to let them graze in the old churchyard, a high, open and exposed place that has a sheer drop and backs onto the North Sea. One evening one of the gypsy families, who had taken over the beach donkey concessions from the Fortunes, left one of their sons to look after them. One of the donkeys managed to catch him off-balance and gave the lad a head- butt which pushed him over the cliff edge and into the harbour below. His death was almost instant. Perhaps then it is little wonder that later that evening I could not sleep!

For almost eight years each morning on holiday was the same. I would walk the dog and collect the newspaper, generally to a backdrop of the seagulls squealing, while mother cooked breakfast and father got dressed and shaved.

Sometime in the 1970s the entire family, apart from father, rebelled and refused to go back to Whitby. A number of alternatives were discussed and eventually Blackpool became the favoured destination. But father rebelled and refused to go on holiday at all, so my mother, brother and sister and I would go away while he stayed at home. Many years later he relented, but only if I would look after the donkeys.

On the first occasion my parents booked a holiday, father phoned in a distressed state to say that unless I helped him fit some locks to the access cover that led into the false roof of his house, he would not be going away – as the neighbours in the adjoining cottage might rob him! I therefore spent one of my precious Saturday mornings fitting trapdoor locks under father's direction, just to keep him happy. The fact that there was nothing worth stealing that would fit through the hatch didn't seem to have dawned on him.

Initially, he had severe reservations about going anywhere that might be termed 'foreign' for his holidays, but as time progressed he became quite relaxed about it all. Some holidays involved travelling on North Sea ferries during November and these ferries even during the summer

In later life father started to enjoy travelling; he is pictured here on the River Rhine.

months can be quite a 'choppy' experience. Father claimed he never suffered sea sickness and took a great delight in eating a hearty cooked buffet breakfast sometimes with double helpings whilst the rest of the passengers felt ill.

After a 24-hour crossing to the Spanish port of Santander his chosen way of communicating with the local bar manager was to grunt and point, using his horse's head handled walking stick, at beer or brandy or whatever he wanted to drink.

One of his favourite destinations was Southern Ireland and, as might be imagined, the Irish love a character and especially one who likes Ireland. In father's earlier droving days for Frank Kelly he had learnt – by mimicking Kelly – how to speak with a soft Irish accent. Typically, after drinking a few pints of beer or Guinness, father would go native and in some of the rougher pubs he frequented he could pass himself off as an Irishman. I suspect that if some of the locals had realised that he was actually an English Protestant, he might have found himself thrown through one of the pub windows!

When father eventually died, the Kerry People newspaper in Killarney, Co. Kerry, ran his obituary on page five and the paper's owner even wrote a personal letter of condolences to mother. Not bad for an English holiday-maker – albeit a rather eccentric one!

Chapter 12

Donkeys to Knaresborough – and breakouts

During the autumn of 1966, and with no prior notice, a letter arrived asking my father to vacate the land at the petrol dump forthwith. It later transpired that the reason father was being given his marching orders was that one of the workers at the dump wanted to keep horses there. The letter shocked father to the core and added further to his worries and mounting paranoia.

Our mother – as nearly always when push came to shove – came up trumps. Surplus land for rent had been spotted at the entrance to Knaresborough and, after a few phone calls and letters from her, a lease was agreed. The owner of the land was Viscountess Constance Macintosh of Halifax, whose family had made their fortune from toffee production in York. From subsequent knowledge, it would seem that the family had bought the land on Harrogate Road just to protect their bedroom views!

The land was already well-known to father because, when he had worked for Kelly as a drover, they had used it as the evening resting place for the various cattle they were taking to farm markets. Over the subsequent years, following the agreement of a lease, the land which was just under ten acres in size, became the linchpin of the donkey business.

Father was particularly proud that the land was on lease to him and his successors, something that he felt was the formal start of the family business. A great deal of effort was made in the early days to fence the land properly and to drain it. Part of the problem was that the area had been ignored for many years and was badly overgrown with thistles and other weeds. Many of the gutters had collapsed and the land drains had fallen into disrepair. To solve the drainage problem, he had a pair of copper rods made, which he held aloft and these would cross as he walked over an underground drain pipe. Water divining had come to Knaresborough!

Meanwhile, within a matter of weeks, the donkeys were quickly munching their way through the thistles and an effort was being made to ensure the fences held good to prevent the animals straying.

Complementary to fencing was the erection of a series of outbuildings. The first of these was a lean-to steel shed that had been a former

Second World War air-raid shelter. The shelter had been donated by Benny White, a Starbeck-based butcher who was also Gerald Walker's employer. Mr White was a kindly man and also handed over other items, including an expensive glass furniture cabinet, which took pride of place in the Allott household, and is now in the possession of my brother Raymond.

The steel shelter was very strong and provided accommodation for up to eight donkeys. In winter it kept the animals dry and in the summer it stopped the flies pestering them. Hay was put in a steel rack at one corner and the donkeys would gather round and take what they could.

Drinking water for the animals was provided from a rising spring, which was subsequently piped by father and fed into a series of small stone troughs. A number of metal water pipes were tied together and fastened to some of the fence stakes in the bottom field adjacent to the small metal lane gate. These would subsequently be used for securing the donkeys when they were being groomed prior to racing.

A great deal of time was spent by father repairing and erecting new barbed-wire fences. Old gates were restored and tarred to provide better access. A steel pipe was also placed between the first and second fields to enable motor vehicles to travel from one to the other. On-going field restoration work was spread over many years. Some of the later work, like the repair of the old lane, did not get completed until around 1975.

While the fencing and farming work was on-going, the donkeys were allowed to run freely. The top field was within 30 yards of Knaresborough golf course and it did not take long for the donkey herd's best escape artists, Jack and Sooty, to figure a way out. Unfortunately it was late autumn and the top part of the golf course had been newly seeded in readiness for the following season. The two donkeys, probably attracted by the unusual bright green colour of the grass, forced themselves out of the field early one morning onto the newly seeded greensward and wandered around.

At around 10am father arrived to give his donkeys hay and noticed that two of his animals were missing. A search of the fields led him to a broken piece of fence and a set of hoof marks leading to the golf course. He quickly shouted to the donkeys "kway, kway, kway" which meant it was hay feeding time, so they had better come quickly. Not surprisingly both animals came trotting. What the golf club groundsman must have thought when he found two sets of hoof prints leading down the newly seeded course I cannot think. Father quickly nailed-up the damaged fence and went home to read a book.

The biggest Knaresborough donkey breakout which subsequently became known as 'The Great Escape', happened after someone with a

Philip with the donkeys at the fields on Harrogate Road. This was originally taken for a newspaper around 1968 with the strapline 'This Boy has 14 Donkeys to Ride'. Father refused to be in the picture because he suffered bouts of camera shyness.

grudge against my father opened the front field gate and shooed all the donkeys onto the A59 in the direction of Knaresborough High Street.

Over the years, Knaresborough police had got used to the odd escaping donkey and to a variety of more exotic animals emigrating from the Knaresborough Zoo. However, the solitary night-duty police officer patrolling the High Street thought he was seeing double – or rather more than that – when 20 donkeys galloped past Woolworths, heading towards the bus station!

A panic call to the police station prompted a 3am call to father to collect his donkeys from the High Street or face some obscure stock management charge.

He arrived on the scene with his van and gave the donkeys a big toot on the horn. The donkeys all knew his old van, having made various journeys in the back. In fact some of the animals, which tried to climb in the front, were probably as familiar with how to drive the vehicle as father was, and when he was drunk possibly nearly as competent!

Donkeys are strange creatures and like humans they don't like a lot of stress. Relieved that father was now present they steadily trotted behind the familiar Ford Thames van as it slowly made its way to the field. When word went around what had happened, father quickly got nicknamed the donkey piper of Knaresborough!

Chapter 13

The Roundabout

In 1967, father purchased a small fold-up roundabout from some dealers in Leeds. The manually-operated unit had been used by gypsies for giving rides on the streets of the city and was in a very poor state of repair. In particular, it looked as if the painting of the different children's toys that decorated the roundabout had been done with a shovel. Thick, ugly, and discoloured old paint covered many of the seats and there were a number of holes in the panels that folded up after use. Two weeks were devoted to restoring it, and when it emerged newly painted in bright red, yellow and black from Mrs Todd's old garage, few people would have realised the dreadful condition it had arrived in.

The roundabout had a bright collapsible umbrella, with a multi-coloured canopy top and a tubular frame. The canopy and frame were specially made for father by two separate firms in Leeds. Prior to assembling the umbrella, he spent three days just painting the tubular frame.

Permission was quickly obtained to put the roundabout in Bilton Fields and an extra notice board was painted to promote it. When the roundabout was not required it could be quickly folded down, and during the summer it was stored under an old tarpaulin cover. It would then be placed in a corner of the wooden fencing that in those days fully surrounded the entrance to Bilton Fields.

On one occasion a group of young lads decided to strip off the cover and fiddle with the machine. Unfortunately for them, father was passing in his van just as they were lifting off the cover. The van was quickly halted and one lad was clipped around the ear and the other had father's size-11 boot thrust into a rather sensitive place.

However, vandalism was not the biggest problem father faced with the roundabout. The biggest issue was finding someone to work it. To solve this dilemma he ended up making a series of temporary arrangements, which resulted over the years, in some rather odd characters being called in to operate it. These included someone who thought he was a secret agent, an alleged hard-man, an ex-convict, an ex-farmhand with emphysema and, of course, Selby John. I felt none of these characters were suited to entertaining small children on the roundabout.

As mentioned earlier in the book, Selby John was its first main operative. Father had met Selby when he was helping to build new houses in

Left to right, Selby John and Ken Mothersill, the cattle wagon driver. The roundabout folded up so that it could be towed by a horse or a car. The picture was taken on Bogs Lane.

Bogs Lane by pushing a wheelbarrow upside down with cement on it! He lived in a lodging house on Skipton Road, in Harrogate and as a young boy I was forbidden by father to go into the property, because he said it would have bugs bigger than donkeys.

Selby was a simple soul and he stuck with father for many years. The fact that the roundabout always made about £3 each day, rain or shine, never seemed to perplex father and the matter never got formally raised with Selby during his long employment. It was only later when someone else operated the roundabout that father discovered it was capable of taking £12 per day!

For many years my sister, brother and I would be regularly forced to go on the wretched thing, often as many as six or seven times a day. Our father's aim was to show other children how wonderful it was in the hope of attracting them. However, the bumpy ride and constant spinning made us all feel quite queasy, and rather than acting as a magnet to other kids, we must – with our face-pulling and sickliness – have put many of them off.

Originally the roundabout had been towed by horse round the streets of Leeds and father, in one of his get-rich-quick schemes, had decided to convert it so it could be towed behind the van. The idea was relatively simple; father and Selby would take it to the council estates in winter to give rides. However, after a few trips, it quickly became apparent that no-one on the estates had much money and the project was, like many others, soon shelved.

Chapter 14

Donkeys up the Dales

The autumn was always a demanding time. Donkey derbies and riding at Bilton Fields stopped promptly at the end of September and the end of the season generally resulted in my parents, brother, sister and myself all having a week's holiday in Whitby (see chapter 11). Returning from Whitby was always a bit depressing – this was the time of year when my father lent out the bulk of his donkeys for the winter.

To get things moving mother would nearly always place an advert in the Yorkshire Post and the Harrogate Advertiser, saying simply: "Winter homes wanted for donkeys". A variety of different people would respond to the advert, some of them horse owners who wanted a donkey to keep a mare company and others, such as farmers who got one for their children to ride.

Typically, they got the benefit of a pet donkey and father got the animal fed. In the majority of cases the arrangement worked extremely well and the same donkey often went back to the same place year after year. On the downside, most of these poor donkeys had to endure being pushed into the back of father's van and carted off, often high up into the Yorkshire Dales to some back-of-beyond farm, that apart from the local postman, no-one had heard of.

Not all donkeys enjoyed the experience and almost without exception they left a large smelly heap of manure in the van, which later had to be swilled out. Some of the more playful donkeys would push at the driver's seat in the hope of dislodging him. Given that the vans had side-opening doors and that the Dales can have somewhat hilly terrain (father always refused to wear a seat belt) it seems miraculous that father was never pushed over the edge, and that all the donkeys got to their destinations.

Before the donkeys could be lent out, a lot of preparation work was needed. The donkeys had to be wormed, liberally doused with louse powder to ensure any parasites were killed and have their hooves trimmed and oiled.

Much of the preparation work, particularly cutting of the hooves, fell on me as the eldest child. This was because after 1963 father had to cut the hooves of the donkeys German-style, this involved someone holding the hoof whilst the farrier does the cutting. The reason for this was due to the fact that father could not bend his left leg, following the earlier van accident. Holding the hoof required someone reasonably strong whilst it was cut. Personally, I always found this time of year extremely stressful because father would sometimes spend the afternoon waiting for school to end. In those days the pubs in Knaresborough closed at about three o'clock, but on the two market days, livestock auction day on Monday and market stalls on Wednesday, various pubs remained open until four o'clock in the afternoon.

He would be at home, generally fairly tanked up on beer, waiting for us all to arrive back from school. It was always the same: "Come on lad, we have work to do". I would be urged to change out of my school uniform and then bundled into the van. At this stage, he would be smoking some heavy tobacco such as 'St Bruno' or 'Condor Ready Rubbed' in his pipe. This was a deliberate strategy aimed at throwing even the most astute police officer off the fact that he had recently drunk quite a few beers!

The van would gently follow the white lines as it made its way to the Harrogate Road fields. Once up the tatty entrance lane, instructions would be given by father as to which of the donkeys had to be caught – normally three or four, who would then be tied up in a neat row. The first animal would have its hooves cleaned out by me, and then father would expect me to hold the first hoof while he started cutting it with a sharp knife and hammer. After cutting the hoof gently, about half an inch would have been removed and father would then file the foot level using a rasp. Each hoof took roughly six minutes to cut, therefore around 25 minutes a donkey to process.

In the early days of father's business, George Collier had taught him the skills of a blacksmith. George used to come twice a year to cut the donkeys' hooves. He was very knowledgeable and taught him numerous trade secrets. George charged five shillings a donkey (25 pence in new money), per hoof. When he retired, he gave his tools to my father. Doing these blacksmith-type jobs saved my father a considerable amount of money and occasionally even provided a source of income when local dignitaries called upon him to attend to their own donkeys.

Holding the donkeys hooves was hard work and normally undertaken by one of the donkey boys. However, after some big bust-up with one of them, father asked me to help. At the age of eleven, I was still not sufficiently strong to hold the hoof as father's blows with the hammer hit down on the blade. At around this time two girls who lived at the high end of the Broadacres Estate, in Harrogate, came to help with the donkeys. Their mother Audrey, got involved in helping and made a small box that a donkey's hoof could be placed in. The unit was used for a number of years and even earned Audrey, courtesy of father, a free trip to Barnaby Horse Fair.

Cutting the donkey's hooves was never a pleasant job. They smelled and in addition, the animals would often push their luck with their behaviour; sometimes pushing, shoving and even relieving themselves! It was not uncommon for misbehaving donkeys to be hit on their backsides by my father a few times with the rasp. It was equally not uncommon for the donkey to try and kick my father, an action which would lead to a swearing fit. The donkeys quickly learned not to muck around, but it was always a different story with celebrities who owned a donkey. In such cases, dad would urge the owner to go off and make a cup of tea and, once out of the way, the donkey would be given a complete telling off and even occasionally hit with the rasp. The returning surprised owner would often comment how well behaved the donkey was and how my father had a way with animals. Frankly, we were very lucky that the animals could not speak.

The preparations for lending out the donkeys were spun out over many evenings in early October. Once each donkey had been processed, a tatty old bridle would be made up and matched with one of the racing pads, which would then have stirrups, and, in many cases, irons fitted. Saturdays and Sundays throughout October were devoted entirely to delivering the donkeys to their new temporary owners, often located in the remote Yorkshire Dales.

Unless the farmer had his own transport such as a horsebox or Land Rover and trailer, the delivery vehicle would be my father's van, with one of Mapplebeck's cattle trucks being called into use, for the longer journeys. Father made a wooden ramp for getting donkeys into the back of his vans. Most of the vans were quite small in the early days, and one even had side windows that the donkeys took a delight in smashing.

A typical Saturday morning would begin with a breakfast of bacon and eggs at around 8.30am, followed by the two of us going to the fields at nine o'clock. A donkey would be caught and pushed up the wooden ramp into the back of the van, and then driven off. Often these trips involved going up mountainous roads, while dad told one of his little stories and smoked his pipe. Before long the old van would mist up and the donkey would get bored. If two had been put in, they might begin fighting each other or worse, they would panic. It was quite common for the donkeys to relieve themselves either by urinating or leaving a big heap of sloppy manure behind. The smell was particularly bad in spring when the donkeys were collected from the farms, as some of them had been fed on winter silage.

Donkeys poking their heads out of the back of father's van became a familiar sight in Knaresborough and helped earn him the nickname of Donkey Dave. One particular journey is still etched on my mind. The van, complete with a donkey in the back, was being driven at around 25 miles an hour when it suddenly veered sideways as it went round a bad bend. The cause of this unexpected movement was the donkey, who for some unknown reason had got in a rage and pushed its head into the front of the van. The donkey gave father a violent nudge and pushed him onto the steering wheel. It also succeeded in snapping my father's pipe and as a consequence it got an absolute rollicking. It had a lucky escape not to have been sent to the cat food-processing factory, which was one of father's favourite threats.

Most of the farms which took the donkeys were quite small owner-manager affairs and were in some cases impoverished, but the hospitality given by the more remote farms was superb. After the donkey had been disembarked and the tack placed in some outhouse, we would generally be invited to take our Wellington boots off and join the family in the parlour. Lavish amounts of teacakes, scones and various other home-made produce would be offered to us, together with large pots of tea. Personally I hated these occasions because at that time I was incredibly wary of eating buttered items that other people had prepared.

After discussions that could go on for an hour, we would be shown around the farm by the proud farmer who would often go into great detail about what he was growing, what arable acres he had and what livestock he was keeping.

Father enjoyed these occasions for it enabled him to talk with some authority and knowledge based on his own farming background. He would often advise farmers about livestock keeping, especially where pigs and sheep were involved.

After what seemed an eternity, we would return to the van and head back down to Knaresborough. Depending on the time of day, we would either call back at Park Place for some lunch, or continue working until the last donkey for that day was ferried off to a farm at around 4pm. By this stage the van would often be a smelly mess and the last donkey would be very reluctant to go into the vehicle, let alone us! Where force was needed, the poor donkey would be yanked in, the ramp lifted and the back doors locked.

The loading and disembarking of the donkeys took place in the lane that ran parallel to the fields. Unfortunately the access was shared with the Welch family, who owned the adjoining land.

In the early days they made a living from providing car parking on busy Bank Holidays and Sundays. During the 1960s there was an element of friction between the Allotts and the Welchs over access to the lane. On one occasion dad was busy loading a donkey into the van when a member of their family wanted to get access to his fields. Needless to say, a great amount of cursing took place, with my father playing the lead role and our relationship with our neighbours became even more strained. This ended in the Welchs attempting to block off father's access by fencing over a metal gate that he had earlier inserted into the lane. After a period of unpleasantness, harmony returned and the matter was left to rest until the following spring.

By the end of October the majority of donkeys had been lent out, although a small residue of perhaps three or four were always left to spend the winter at home. These generally comprised what we called the Motley Crew – animals that were sick or elderly or which were not suitable for lending out because of inherent defects such as continually throwing off the rider and then jumping on him or her! The Motley Crew was always sent up to Bogs Lane for the winter, which gave the land at Knaresborough a rest and allowed it to recover from the heavy summer grazing.

As the winter evenings drew in, father would start his land maintenance routine at Knaresborough. This included cutting hedges, digging out gutters, trapping moles, removing thistles and cutting up the tree stumps. Weather permitting, this would continue, with the odd lull for Yarm fair and Christmas, until the February school half-term.

Chapter 15

Yarm Fair

During the month of October each year, money permitting – and it was not always the case that he was well-off enough – my father would 'escape' for a few days to Yarm Fair, one of the North's top horse, pony and donkey events. He would, where possible, equip one of his old vans with a bed, kettle, primus stove, curtains and the basic, rudimentary items needed for 'camping', including an old black wooden chest filled with food, and then he would be off.

Yarm is a traditional Northern market town with cobbled streets and unusually is bordered by two rivers. These comprise the River Tees in the north, and the Levan to the east. Historically Yarm was the highest port on the River Tees and merchant vessels used to travel up the tidal river from the North Sea to trade.

Its fair is one of the biggest in its calendar and owes its origins to an event for farmers to trade in cheese and livestock. It now combines a gypsy-style horse show with a fairground that brings the centre of the town alive for five nights from Tuesday to Saturday normally in the third week of October. Horse trading still takes place at the lower end of the town, with the upper part being reserved for the fairground rides and amusements, which are largely geared towards a teenage audience and there are also attractions for youngsters.

Wherever possible father generally preferred to be accompanied on his visit to the fair and his fellow traveller would normally be one of those who had helped him with the donkeys through the summer. Past companions have included Gerald Walker, Bob Scurr and Norman Mothersill. Yarm is an annual event and father would often spend more money on beer than on food. Father would set up camp towards the top end of the Main Street, as near as he could get to the railway bridge – an old-fashioned iron bridge which carried the Darlington and Stockton Railway that was made famous by George Stephenson and his Rocket.

Not that camping close to the railway had anything to do with father being a train buff, or anything remotely like that. No, but there was a certain irrefutable logic to it when the lack of sanitary and hygiene facilities at horse fairs in those days is taken into account. There were bushes beneath the viaduct arches and these afforded excellent cover when used as toilet facilities. It was far from unusual to see a number of gypsies

The Black Bull pub, one of the pubs where father spent his time drinking during Yarm Fair

disappearing in there armed with the previous day's newspaper, even though the majority of them could not read!

Yarm was then a town well provided with pubs, and these were put to exceptionally good use over the fair days. Hostelries included the Black Bull and the Kenton Ox, or the 'Kettnox' as father would call it. The reason he gave it a fresh name was because 'Kettnox' was sometimes used as a sort of gypsy slang for 'don't say anything' – the proper gypsy word is pronounced 'keck'. This might not have been so bad had father put the saying into practice. But as the drink flowed, he tended to get more boisterous and to impart more and more 'wisdom' to other fairgoers.

It had long been an ambition of mine to join father on one of his trips to Yarm and, as a young child of five, I remember crying bitterly when he refused to take me. I could only watch as one of his helpers climbed aboard the van instead. I was hardly placated by being assured I was staying at home, not because he did not want me with him, but because of the conditions encountered there. And it is true that at times the fair could be incredibly rough.

When I reached the age of 10, father relented and he and I rode forth in his Ford Thames van which, as usual, had been roughly kitted-out for camping and had curtains at its side windows. Once we arrived, I was given money to go on the rides with the provision that I returned to the van at 9pm. Father, meanwhile, drank until closing time before stumbling back.

I remember that on the first day everything went without a hitch, but on the second night father had just returned and we had settled for the night when a gang began to shake the van violently.

Looking through a crack in the curtains father spied three ugly-look-ing lads, obviously bent on causing trouble. He shouted at them, words to the effect of 'Time for you to go home ... so piss off now' but it all had little effect.

However, drunk or sober, father was never a man to trifle with. The kettle was put on to boil and a van starting handle was pulled free from its storage place beneath the front seat. Father told me that I had to pour boiling water over the feet of the youths, while he smacked them with the starting handle.

So he pulled back the curtains in preparation for our attack and began to psych them up with words like 'You twats have had it' or some such phrase, along with various other unrepeatable expletives.

When they saw father's face the youths, who were all gypsies, were somewhat shocked. For not only did they recognise him, they knew him as a friend of their father's. This brought an instant end to their trou-ble-making without having to resort to our planned violence. The first gypsy youth apologised and promised father a white pup in the morning as a peace offering. The second youth also apologised and offered to return with two coloured pups. The third apologised too, but then ran off into the night. The rest of the night passed off peacefully so we never had to use the boiling water and starting handle treatment.

The following day, in good heart, father invited one of his gypsy friends over for morning coffee. The problem with that was that father was completely unused to the proprieties of handing out morning coffee and most gypsies, of course, are far from accustomed to receiving it. But father duly boiled the kettle before dispensing the contents into an elderly porcelain cup. Unfortunately for father and particularly for his gypsy guest, the handle fell off and boiling water poured down the poor chap's trousers, causing injuries which were severe enough for him to undergo a brief spell of hospitalisation. After this experience, he stuck to having smoke breaks with his gypsy friends, ruling that they were less dangerous than making morning coffee!

Father was fond of using the Romany tongue at events like the Yarm Fair. I remember him saying to me in front of some gypsy lads: "Del and get mandy some tulvors and ticknor can have a colum." Which roughly translates as: "Go and get father some cigarettes and you can have a shil-ling (five pence)."

The lads who heard what was said were taken aback at the fact that not only could he speak Romany, but I could understand what he was saying. They looked at each other in puzzlement and it was clear that they did not understand what had been said!

Our trip to Yarm should have provided father with the ideal opportu-nity to buy some donkeys and harnesses, but this seldom proved to be the case. However, he always had a damned good time and this often led to him spending his very last penny on 'entertaining' at the fair. Many of his friends had little or no money but when he had the cash he would happily buy them drinks and keep them entertained. Once, however, this generosity backfired in more ways than one.

In the excitement of being at Yarm – and with all the drinking which had gone on – father had forgotten to put petrol in the van for the return journey. In the days before credit cards this was a somewhat dangerous and foolhardy thing to do, especially when you have spent your last penny. But as far as father was concerned there was no problem. Lack of petrol could be easily remedied. The solution he hit on comprised a gallon of paraffin and a container of methylated spirits. Both were poured into the petrol tank and – strangely – seemed to work well enough. At least until we reached Boroughbridge where the engine boiled over and brought a memorable end to the first time I camped with father at Yarm Fair!

Chapter 16

Winters

It was not uncommon in October for people like Selby John and other simple folk who helped with the donkeys, to be engaged by father to do the farm work. Selby was particularly good at digging out hedge gutters (small dykes that often run alongside Yorkshire field boundaries), possibly because of his previous employment as a building labourer. He could dig straight trenches for miles, until he was either distracted by some local event such as an accident or because father could no longer fund him. On one occasion he was left to sort out the front gutter adjoining the Harrogate roadside, while father retired to take refreshments at the George Hotel. However, a 1950s Volkswagen Beetle that was travelling at speed down Harrogate Road, lost control of the highway, crossed the central white line and rolled over onto its side onto the raised soft grass verge just above the front donkey field. Its driver (who must have experienced this problem before), just tipped it back over onto its wheels with the help of a pedestrian and with the car now backfiring, continued his journey down the road. This sight greatly frightened Selby John who travelled everywhere by bus and did not even hold a driving licence, let alone own a car. Panicking, he ran down the road and refused to work for the rest of the day. On these types of occasions father was incredibly understanding and supplied Selby – not to mention himself – with liberal amounts of alcohol before bundling him on the bus to Harrogate.

By the end of October my assistance was limited to helping on Saturdays, unless of course there was a family emergency. Winter Saturdays were grim affairs, as by now the weather was very cold and I was expected to help cut up wood. Much of the timber consisted of fallen tree trunks, which were often quite substantial and needed splitting first with metal wedges. The wood, often still wet from the mud and rain, was subsequently placed, after cutting, into mucky old hemp sacks.

This work generally took two or three hours until we had filled at least a couple of sacks with logs, which would normally be sufficient to supply the household for the following week.

Normally, we had father's van and the sacks of wood would be loaded in and transported home. However, for a couple of winters he went into economy mode and would carry a small sack all the way from the Harrogate Road to Park Place, in his Wellington boots and mucky old overcoat.

While following behind I once heard a young child get extremely excited and shout to his own father: "Look, daddy, there's a dirty old tramp". Fortunately my own father kept his mouth closed on the expletives he could easily have off-loaded, and continued on the journey home.

The cold, coupled with the strenuous work, was very demanding on everyone and as I got older I came to hate winter Saturdays.

When father owned a van, the vehicle would be backed up to the small wall running adjacent to Park Place. Then the sacks could be quickly lifted over and placed in one of the outhouses that faced the backyard at Park Place.

This was always embarrassing to me due to the fear that school friends might be passing by and might see the humiliating circumstances that my family and myself lived in.

Occasionally, the Saturday task of collecting firewood would be cancelled in favour of a trip to see nearby relatives. During the winter my parents would try to visit their relations at least once. For mother – and later Katherine, Raymond and me – this meant a trip to Leeds to see her parents along with her Aunt Lillian and husband George.

Sadly, mother's own mum died prematurely in the mid-1960s from cancer and so after grandfather remarried we would go to see Auntie Phyllis and Grandfather Anderson.

When father had a roadworthy vehicle, a trip to Darington to visit Uncle Osmond and also the Kirks was mandatory. Apart from these trips few other journeys were ever undertaken in winter, due to the financial cost.

Father was very good at story telling and whilst my brother, sister and I were small, this was great fun. Time permitting during these winter months he would patiently read to us on an evening before we went to bed. Each of the children was given a favorite story, Raymond's was 'Fantastic Mr Fox'. The book was not unlike Roald Dahl's version but customised by father. Katherine had 'Lost at the Fair' but with the characters names changed to those of other family members and neighbours.

My own book was 'Downey Duck', which was about a family of ducks. During the early part of our childhood having these stories read was great fun but as the family got older the stories started to become a little tiresome. This was particularly so after father had had a few drinks during the summer months and started to reminisce.

To generate extra food for the table during the winter, father decided in his wisdom, to start breeding rabbits to eat. This had been triggered by Raymond and me keeping two pet rabbits: one named Benjamin, given to Raymond by a gypsy, and the other named Peter, bought by me from a Knaresborough family.

Father decided that the pet rabbits should be relocated to the land at Harrogate Road. He scrounged a collection of old cabinets and some female rabbits were purchased. The furniture used for the cages came from a variety of sources, including a Latvian chap called Adam who lived nearby.

Within a matter of months the rabbits were happy – and generating lots of offspring which, when fat enough, were liquidated by father and subsequently cooked. As time went on the whole family, apart from father, became bored with eating rabbit, but the stock kept expanding. To meet their feeding requirements, Katherine, Raymond and I were delegated the task of collecting old cabbage bits from Prudames, a local fruit and vegetable shop based in Knaresborough Market Place. Demand however continued to grow and the collection of greens expanded to the other shops such as Crowthers and a succession of smaller shops that came and went in the town centre.

To manage this collection process, father issued us all with large hessian sacks. The embarrassment and humiliation of carrying these around the town after school, often in front of schoolmates, still haunts me today.

There were times when the greengrocers in Knaresborough did not have enough cabbage leaves to meet father's heavy demands, and when this happened I would be despatched to the Horner brothers for turnips.

The two Horner brothers lived with their sister on the Wetherby Road, running into Harrogate. Their farm has since been converted into a themed pub called The Kestrel, but when I used to call as a schoolboy, it was a working farm. To collect the turnips and sometimes mangle-wurzels (a root crop grown and often fed to sheep), I was given three hessian sacks and a steel carrier bike.

The carrier bike had belonged to a local grocer and had a small wheel at the back and a metal stand for parking at the front. It had no gears and, when loaded with three sacks of turnips, was incredibly hard to manoeuvre, let alone pedal. The journey to the farm was around two-and-a-half miles and required me to travel along Briggate, the steepest road in the town. The return journey was along Waterside and it took all the strength I could muster just to push the bike along the flat road. On arrival father would generally greet me with some sarcasm, such as: "Where have you been lad, I thought you had emigrated."

The keeping of rabbits needless to say continued for only a few years, as the lack of interest by the rest of the family in eating them eventually persuaded father to call a halt and let them all go!

Despite the toughness of the winters and our lack of money, father always had time for society's less fortunate people. On a Sunday, people like Jim Taylor and Tom Dawson, who both lived alone, would be invited round in the evening for tea or coffee and sometimes a light meal. For people like Tom, who had lived on Welch's Caravan Park until the local authority forced him to move to a house, this provided interaction with other people. Often the conversation with Tom and Jim would go on for a few hours until father got bored with their company and he would then start to ignore them and read his book.

The highlight of the winter months was Christmas and our parents would save up what little money they had and when possible they would buy us all decent presents. Each Christmas would follow a similar format with my brother, sister and me getting up in the early hours of the morning to open all our gifts. Father would then put on a record at high volume and put the speakers against the adjoining wall of one of the neighbour's cottages. Father said this was to pay them back for all the banging and noise they had made during the year, but somehow I don't think they saw it that way.

Father would feed the donkeys that were wintering at home mid-morning, while mother worked away preparing and then cooking the turkey. Lunch would be served promptly at 1pm, followed by crackers and pudding. After lunch, the family would play with their presents or party games while father would have a couple – or more – whiskies and eventually fall noisily to sleep.

On each dry Boxing Day, father, Jack Barrass, myself and Jill the dog would normally go rabbiting. In the early days this involved the use of ferrets and nets to trap the rabbits on the petrol dump, because due to the storage of fuel onsite, guns were forbidden for risk that they could create a fire and even an explosion.

In later years father and Jack would shoot with permission on the Welch property and on our own land. They both always took a very sporting view and would only fire at rabbits or pheasants if they were moving.

Animals that they shot would be hung in the coal shed for a few days to game up, then skinned, with the surplus being put into the freezer for the New Year. Father and mother would normally start the New Year with a few sherries, nothing very grand because in winter they were always short of funds. The longer winter days of January would be used by father for harness repairs, other essential maintenance tasks and lots of reading.

Chapter 17

Preparing for Summer

January dragged into February and then it was on to the school half-term break. This was particularly important because it was the time of year that father cleaned all the donkey harnesses, with the help of a number of young people and my own efforts. The work was generally tackled with great enthusiasm by all except me – in anticipation of the donkeys giving their first rides of the season at Easter.

Please forgive me if this all sounds a little 'schoolish,' but the family business revolved around school children. This is because the majority of helpers were at school, and nearly all the customers went to school. In those days the pubs closed at 3pm in Knaresborough with some serving for an extra hour on the two market days. This convenient coincidence meant that during the summer father could indulge in his two great passions in life, drinking and donkeying, without the two clashing. More often than not I would arrive home from school to find father half-drunk and expecting help with the donkeys.

The number of vehicles he banged, dented and wrote-off between the hours of 3.30pm and 4.30pm takes all the fingers of both hands to count them on – and that is just for the days when I was present!

During the spring half-term, all the harnesses would be taken down from various remote household locations, such as the tops of dusty wardrobes, in preparation for cleaning. This consisted of a number of processes involving neatsfoot oil, saddle soap and either Brasso or Silvo, two metal polishes. Damaged harnesses would be repaired and then coloured black using specialist leather dye.

The servicing of the harness in the early days took place in the old bus body that father called his saddle room at Bogs Lane. Later, following the building of sectional sheds, this work would be transferred to the land at Knaresborough. From the mid-1960s the majority of work in preparation for the coming season was completed at Bogs Lane, with the remainder taking place at Park Place.

Firstly, all bridles were stripped-down; buckles were cleaned with the appropriate metal cleaner and then polished. Hot neatsfoot oil was painted into the rough side of the leather and saddle soap was then applied to the finished side, using a soft cloth. Each bridle also had a number of metal studs, which were very time-consuming to clean, as they had to be individually polished.

Every three years father gave each of the donkeys' headbands and nosebands a fresh coat of bright red (ex-Post Office) paint, and each donkey's name was painted in white on the distinctive headband. In the 1950s and 1960s Gerald Walker undertook the actual name painting. But in the later years, father started doing it himself, though in all honesty the presentation was never quite the same.

The majority of the donkeys had their own individual bridle, although in a number of cases new donkeys would take over an old name such as Sooty, as father would not create a new name band if it was still a popular name. The naming of donkeys was a rather strange affair. In essence the rule was that if the donkey had been troublesome, such as the original Sooty, then it was OK to replace it with a new donkey called Sooty. This normally took place after the original donkey had been sold, died or been put down and sent off to a canning factory to be turned into cat food!

Conversely, if father thought a donkey had worked hard – such as Muffin or Punch – then that name would cease after the donkey was taken out of service. You would have thought it would have been the other way round! This hit-and-miss policy generated a large number of surplus headbands which would litter the saddle room for years to come, until father had one of his big cleanouts.

Names chosen for the donkeys were mostly from popular radio and television programmes. So Muffin came from TV's *Muffin the Mule*, and Silver from the "Hi Ho Silver" cry of *The Lone Ranger*, a 1950s cowboy series. Leo came from the Walt Disney production *Leo the Lion*. These names were generally at least twenty years out of date, although in fairness to the kids who came to ride them, they never seemed to care.

The maximum number of donkeys father could use for providing rides was governed by the number of bell collars and saddles he had. Including the side-saddle, 13 saddles could be mustered and around the same number in silver and brass bell collars. The saddles were all equipped with red handles made from those which had once adorned metal buckets which had outlived their usefulness. A similar cleaning policy used for the bridles was also extended to the saddles and this generally resulted in a residue of saddle soap being left on the seats. Father found this rather funny and said he enjoyed the saddles being polished by little arses as it not only generated money, but saved everyone the task of actually polishing them. I suspect that countless children must have been chastised after their Easter donkey ride for trouser-stain mishaps, which were not of their own making.

Out of the three different types of harness, it was the collars which created the most interest. The collars all had matching bells, either Victorian brass or a cheaper chrome version. Each was painted red and equipped with four bells that rang as the donkey walked and ran. Cleaning them was a pain as the Brasso often spilt onto the red collar leaving a dirty brass or silver stain. The number of times I was scolded or clipped for spilling onto the collar doesn't bear thinking about.

For donkey racing, father had sixteen felt pads. These stayed in place on the donkey through a single girth and tail cropper. The preparation of the pads would take place at a separate time, as the donkey derby season did not start until nearly Whitsuntide.

By the end of the half-term week the majority of tack would have been cleaned and father would then, if necessary, paint the notice boards and seat. The seat was a bench-type, ex-army seat folded flat for easy carrying after use at the riverside. This was painted yellow so that, according to father, it would show up in the grass and not be lost.

Chapter 18

The Riverside

On most days that children were on school holidays during the summer months, father would bring his donkeys down to the riverside on an afternoon to give rides. Getting the donkeys to the riverside and back home afterwards was always stressful because each journey required the donkeys to be led across the busy A59. This inevitably would sometimes bring father into conflict with thoughtless local motorists who would sometimes drive too close or even toot their horns. Motorists doing so were liable to get a good cursing or, in extreme cases, get their cars hit with a big knobbly stick which he nearly always carried. He would also proudly lecture these motorists, and anyone else who would listen, that his animals had priority because they were blessed by Jesus and that they were around before cars had even been invented. Sensible motorists didn't argue with him!

During these summer months father considered himself the king of the castle down at the riverside and would often take it upon himself to get involved with matters that had nothing to do with him. This all originated back in the days when Charles Hubert Blenkhorn had the first lot of pleasure boats nearest to the High Bridge. Hubert was the oldest operator down by the river and he and father became very good friends, even taking the odd day trip to Whitby together. Hubert looked just like a ship's captain, due to his ruby face, white beard and boat cap. Not surprisingly, in Whitby he was mistaken for a newly arrived boat captain, which caused some amusement.

Discussions between Hubert, father and other business associates such as Edward Whiteman, a Londoner who had a snack bar in Conyngham Hall car park, took place after work in the World's End pub. When Hubert died in 1966, his son Dick Blenkhorn took over the boats and the business continued in much the same fashion. The death of Hubert elevated father's status in the area – at least in his own eyes – and he started to boss the other riverside businesses around. However, nobody seemed to mind. In fact, a number of people such as Bill Metcalfe the Conyngham Hall car park attendant and park ranger, actually looked up to father.

Bill was a kindly bloke who wandered around Macintosh Park in a smock collecting litter. On Sundays Bill also provided parking directions for coach drivers and collected the car park money from a small

Donkeys going home: they had to be led up the hill to nearby fields. Unusually, the wagon driver Jim Brooks is at the front leading them.

wooden hut. During the winter, Bill would repair the little wooden bridges that connected the various riverside parks and sort out any troubles that might arise. Bill was provided with housing accommodation by the council at the entrance to the Conyngham Hall car park, a property which has now been converted into a Chinese restaurant.

During the summer Uncle Bill, as father insisted I call him, collected bottles in the park. In those days, the majority of bottles had a deposit fee, which was repaid on return. Bill would sometimes collect up to a couple of hundred bottles and give them to me before my holiday, so that I could cash them in for spending money.

On occasions when father felt motivated, he would join Bill on his rounds. What Bill lacked in firepower, father more than made up for. Courting couples were told to be more discreet and peeping toms hanging around were thrown out of the park by father, sometimes physically.

I was seven at around this time and father fell into one of his strange drinking patterns that would happen for a few years and then suddenly change. This involved the van being parked up in Conyngham Hall car park during the summer months at around 6.30pm, after he had dropped off the donkey lads in Starbeck. I would then be given about 30 pence to spend at Edward's (Uncle Ted's) snack bar. My purchases would normally comprise a bottle of shandy, a packet of crisps and a packet of Dairylea cheese and crackers. I would eat these in the van while father went into the World's End for what was supposed to be a quick drink but was often quite a lot more. Ted would then close up and I would be left sitting in the van for up to an hour, sometimes even longer, waiting for father to return.

On one occasion a chap with a car came down and started trying to break into Ted's snack bar. I watched from the back of the van for a time before running off to find him in the pub. The man trying to smash his way into the snack bar tried to call me back but I was not in the mood for taking chances and also felt very scared. When alerted to what was happening, father came tumbling out of the pub after me and slapped his hand up in the middle of the road leading out of the car park to stop the thief's getaway.

When father stood tall his height was just short of six foot and I watched with some satisfaction as the car was brought to a skidding halt. There then followed one of father's boring lectures to the bloke on the perils of thieving, which must have lasted for about half an hour. I was hoping all the time for some action and for the police to be called. But father, given his semi-drunk state, was having none of it. After frightening the bloke by telling him what he would do if he caught him down by the river again, father allowed him to drive away, albeit very shaken!

A few years later Ted, who had just finished a drinking session with father, decided to go and check his snack bar before getting the bus to Ripon, where he lived. On checking the vehicle, he noticed that the door was not properly shut and so he gave it a big slam. The snack bar had a leaky gas bottle and the force of the door slamming caused the bottle to ignite, resulting in the roof being blown off.

Ted stood there aghast, while father at full speed hobbled off to collect a fire extinguisher from Blenkhorn's boathouse. Unfortunately for all concerned both extinguishers were past their expiry date and totally useless. Father rather bravely grappled with the flaming gas canister in an attempt to put it into the river but the intensity of the heat was too great.

In Knaresborough up until the early 1970s the only way of alerting the town's retained fire crew was to sound the 'nuclear alert' siren located on the fire station roof. As can be imagined, by the time the fire engine arrived, the snack bar was almost gutted. A few of the food items were salvaged and apparently for once the hot dogs and hamburgers, which were served to the fire crew, were properly cooked!

Father arranged with David Welch, who still had the Dropping Well Farm, for the gutted snack bar to be placed in one of his large farm buildings, pending major repairs. Over the next two weeks, he helped Ted to fit a new plastic roof and other vital fixtures, after which it was repainted yellow. The newly renovated, but still shabby snack bar was then towed back to its original position.

As time went on father fell out with the landlord of the World's End, resulting in him being banned. Meantime Bill and his wife moved out of the Conyngham Hall lodge and their replacements were the Wainmans. Shortly after this, the council decided to install automated barriers to the car park, which rose to let vehicles leave after payment of the appropriate parking fee.

The Wainmans had a young family and it was not long before their daughters Vicky, Tracy and their friend Corrina were helping with the donkeys. As time progressed, father would spend chunks of time talking to Phil Wainman and his wife Pat, on nearly every summer Sunday. At about this time an undesirable man nicknamed Mucky Arthur started hanging around. It was claimed that he had been seen trying to peep into the ladies' toilets, which were on the other side of the road from the car park entrance.

This was now the height of the summer season and the last thing father wanted was some kind of voyeur hanging around. He waited for Arthur to arrive and then pointed gently to the ladies' toilet window and waved his stick. Sensibly, Arthur said he had a headache and went off home claiming to be sick!

At the top part of Bilton Fields was a triangular tarmac area inside the fencing, as already mentioned. This was let on an annual basis as an ice-cream concession to various vendors. These included a Mr J. Symonds of the Adelphi Hotel in Harrogate, Mr W. Gill from a Harrogate trailer park and later C & M Creamery Ices from Grove Park Terrace, Harrogate. My own favourite was C & M because of the large number of free ice creams I got. In return for free ice cream father looked after the Italian couple who owned the business and ensured that none of the day-trippers or locals got the better of them.

At the other side of Harrogate Road is the Dropping Well Estate, once reputedly occupied by Mother Shipton, England's most famous witch. Until a sale in 1986, the Estate was run as a limited company by a family member and director of the business, Shirley MacLean. The estate also owned the Dropping Well Farm which, in the 1980s, was renamed Badger Hill and subsequently sold. Mrs MacLean would occasionally chat to father but for most of the time he kept out of her way.

For many years David Welch was tenant of the Dropping Well Farm and ran a number of businesses from there. Originally he had a dairy farm and later a business called Knaresborough Jack. This evolved around a Cleveland Bay stallion he kept and charged out as a stud. David Welch also had a caravan park tenancy on the farm which dated back to the 1930s. The campers caused father on-going hassle through cutting

Dave Castleton, the landlord of the George Hotel gives Silver the donkey a bottle of beer, whilst David Allott anxiously looks on.

back the adjoining hedges and trespassing. Some of the people like Ken North, a miner, would become friends with father, although the majority of them were ignored.

Over the years, David helped out and, according to father's records, gave him a glowing reference for a Milk Recorder job in the 1950s. In the late 1960s he sometimes took father to the odd horse fair like Appleby and occasionally also lent him a tractor.

David Welch was a strict 'tee-totaller' and when he was giving father a lift home from Appleby, it must have created some friction between them. Mr Welch had three daughters, Ann, Mary and Gale along with two sons, Danny and John. The latter sometimes drank with father in the George Hotel. From the mid-1960s there was a cool atmosphere between them, which had largely been fuelled by the on-going row regarding the access lane, as covered elsewhere in this book.

Around 1973 David Castleton became the new landlord of the George Hotel. David was soon persuaded by father to take him to horse fairs and to also provide him with the odd extra drink outside the then strict licensing hours!

Business was initially slow for the new landlord and so father hit on a marketing idea to boost Dave Castleton's liquor sales. He would bring a donkey into the pub for a bottle of beer. The animal picked was the donkey called Silver, better known as 'kick-em-when-they're-down' due

Apart from a new name the George Hotel, now called the Yorkshire Lass, has changed little over the years.

to his reputation for throwing off the jockeys who rode on him at donkey derbies and then jumping on them.

Arrangements were made for Silver to come in and drink a pint with his owner, so the photographers from the Yorkshire Post, Evening Post and Knaresborough Post could take a picture. On the first occasion, Silver was non-plus about participating, but drank a brown ale nevertheless. The second time he tried a pint, but on the third occasion he had an attack of the wind and left such a mess on the pub carpet that David Castleton never invited him back again.

Around 1978 the George was sold and it changed its named to the Moray Arms, which was promoted as a free house. The new pub owner was Moray Irvine and he wasted little time in claiming the triangular fenced area at the side of his pub. This resulted in the dismantling of the Council-maintained fence and the erecting by Irvine of signage, claiming that he now owned the area.

As can be imagined, father felt threatened and it brewed up into one almighty row. The town council took father's side and Harrogate District Council, which Knaresborough had become a part of in 1974, sympathised with Irvine. After various threats and rows, Irvine became so frightened of father that he would not dare leave the pub when the donkey board was put out.

Once, father did not put the board out and caught Irvine arguing with the elderly C & M ice-cream couple. As retribution, he physically kicked Irvine back into the pub.

Eleven months later, Irvine crossed the road to apologise to father. Irvine said the pub was closing due to outstanding debts and that he would be leaving Knaresborough later that week.

The Moray Arms, now closed, was taken over by John Smith's and sold shortly afterwards to Len Cowen. At this point the pub was renamed the Yorkshire Lass and 18 months later it changed hands again when it was bought by Derek Speirs.

Father continued drinking in the pub until 1993 and his stool is the third on the right when facing the bar. Even today Derek still talks about father and his antics. The fact that Derek is now in possession of the carrier bike that I rode to the Kestrel, plus various other artefacts belonging to the old George Hotel, seems to indicate that father did a rather good selling job.

Chapter 19

The Stallion & Thistle Hill

Whenever possible, father attended the annual Appleby Fair, held each June in the town of Appleby-in-Westmorland, Cumbria. It is one of the best known of the horse fairs attended by gypsy families. They travel great distances to meet up with old friends and to buy and sell animals. Most of the time this annual event was just an opportunity for father to get blind drunk in the company of his gypsy friends. Occasionally a donkey would be offered to father that would meet his very demanding standards and a purchase would be made.

In the summer of 1970 just such a transaction took place. For some years, father had been bemoaning the fact that he could not operate a proper donkey farm without the aid of his own stallion. On this occasion someone had actually brought one to sell, an extremely fine specimen that stood over 12 hands high. The silver and grey donkey was in extremely good health and cut an impressive figure. After some tricky negotiations a purchase price of £50 was agreed with the owner and the transaction was completed.

The task of collecting the donkey was given to Maurice Mapplebeck, who took his cattle wagon over to collect the new prize purchase, while father waited nervously. It was common for people to buy blind or sick animals at the fairs, and given the inebriated state father had been in the day before, he had good cause to be worried.

Initially the new donkey went to Bogs Lane because, as it was mid-summer, no other donkeys were based there and the land had been set aside for producing the annual hay crop. The stallion was given the name Jerry and he was initially tethered on a spare strip of land adjoining the main field. The donkey was incredibly powerful and when I was asked to hold him, he dragged me down a number of times. When this happened, my father would give the donkey a good cursing plus a bit of stick and would then give me a telling-off for being weak.

At around that time one of the other donkeys called Rosy was expecting a foal (father used to borrow a stud stallion). Assisting us on that particular day was one of the dimmer donkey boys. "Big foal isn't it, Mr Allott?" asked the lad. Needless to say, father and I howled with laughter!

Bogs Lane was not really suitable for Jerry because other donkeys would have to be transferred there for the winter and father had no inten-

The stallion donkey spent much of its time based at Thistle Hill, near Knaresborough. This stone-built stable provided the donkey with protection from the elements.

tion of letting Jerry get them in the family way; not after the bad episode in 1963, and not without proper business planning. Therefore father set about looking for a small area of land where Jerry could be permanently based. Eventually, a couple of acres at Thistle Hill were found, near what is now Knaresborough's southern bypass, and negotiations started with the owner in order to finalise a lease agreement.

In the meantime, Jerry stayed up at Bogs Lane and I took a small number of jenny donkeys from the fields on Harrogate Road to be serviced by him. The distance of just over a mile required me to lead each of the mare donkeys along, while father travelled ahead in his van. He would then nearly always chastise me when I eventually arrived, for being so slow.

Summer quickly turned to autumn and still the land at Thistle Hill had not been sorted, primarily due to the price the owner wanted. At around 3am one Sunday morning, the telephone rang at Park Place, which caused something of a rumpus. Father always took the view that if the phone rang late, or early in the morning it was generally because of a death or some kind of disaster. On this occasion it was the police – a donkey was running amok around Knaresborough and the police wanted father to catch it.

Events pieced together afterwards seemed to suggest that Jerry the stallion had heard the donkeys at Harrogate Road braying and had decided to join them. However, a solid six-barred oak gate and just over a mile of public highway, part of the A59, stood in his way.

Jerry therefore decided to run at the gate, which he smashed into eight pieces, before trotting down Harrogate Road. A member of the public saw the donkey running down the road (some people never sleep) and phoned the police.

Two police officers attempted to corner the animal near the Harrogate Road field, although both came off the worst.

One tried to put a rope round the donkey's neck while the other tried to herd it into a nearby field. Jerry was not a donkey to be messed with, and he kicked one police officer into the roadside gutter, before dragging the other down. He then kicked the police car with such force that a permanent hoof mark was left in the door, just next to the word 'police'!

Father quickly got down to Harrogate Road, and put a halter on Jerry, who now was so tired as to offer no resistance to being dragged back to Bogs Lane as quickly as possible. On Monday father was asked to report to Knaresborough Police station to discuss the matter. In theory this was quite a serious incident, involving a dangerous animal being allowed to roam the Queen's highway. Then there was the 'assault' on police officers and finally damage to police property – the patrol car!

Knaresborough is a relatively small town and back in the early 1970s the population was just around 10,000. The police were very embarrassed by the incident and certainly did not want the then West Riding Police headquarters at Wakefield knowing about it, let alone any locals, who would have ridiculed them. So an agreement was reached; father would keep quiet about the incident, relocate the donkey further away and the police would not press charges!

The agreement on the Thistle Hill land was now settled in a matter of days and the donkey was quickly transferred there. For the next few years, this was Jerry's permanent home. In future, donkeys to be put in the family way would have to be dragged along Waterside, a narrow bustling road at the side of the River Nidd, to his field.

The land at Thistle Hill had a stone stable-type building on two acres of farmland which fronted onto the main road. Some renovations were needed to make the stable habitable for Jerry and some old bushes needed cutting down and burning. This work took a few weeks and as usual I was roped-in after school to help.

A stable roof ladder was made and a number of new titles were applied to the roof. A replacement water trough was also installed. The old bushes were cut down and pulled into a bonfire for burning.

Despite the poor state of our family's income, my parents always thought they knew their station. In their eyes they were house-owning, independent folk who ran their own 'Knaresborough Donkeys' business.

While not as successful as many other businesses it still gave them – in their opinion – an elevated status over those who lived in a council house and didn't have two pennies to rub together. This was no more telling than when father decided we would burn the old bushes at the Thistle Hill field one evening straight after school.

A bagful of old newspapers and comics was prepared at home (nothing got wasted). Father and I, dressed in old ripped clothes, travelled in a van which leaked when it rained, occasionally backfired and made constant funny noises, to the Thistle Hill field.

Further up the road past the field, on the same side, was a children's home. At about 4.30pm a number of well-dressed school children began to pass the field. "Look at that," said my father. "Those poor buggers haven't got anything, go stand at the gate and give them some of these comics, as they will be very pleased with them."

Patiently, I stood by the field gate in my mucky jeans, ripped jacket, homemade tatty pullover and leaky Wellington boots in order to offer the children the comics as they passed by. Most of them had better school uniforms than mine and nearly all of them looked at me with a variety of expressions ranging from sadness to disdain. Only a couple of the kids took comics, with the whole exercise taking a humiliating 20 minutes for me to complete.

Afterwards father said, "I bet we made those kids' evening, they don't have a van to travel in and nice comics to read like you!"

Chapter 20

Vans

As we have seen, transport for getting from A to B was nearly always by van in the Allott household. Most of these vehicles were very dilapidated, had large rust sections, wheels that wobbled and back doors that often neither closed properly, nor matched. However, one thing most of these vans did have in common was their ability to transport hay and donkeys as discussed earlier.

From the mid-1960s onwards, father started to buy Ford Thames vans, then Bedfords and, when these all became obsolete, he switched to Transit vans. All were run until they broke down or required large amounts of money spending on them to get them through the MOT. Over a period of time father dumped a series of vans in the fields at Harrogate Road.

Vehicle servicing in the early 70s was normally carried out by J. T. Clapham & Sons, Automobile Engineers, on York Place. The garage, which is now flats, was one of those old-fashioned places that also had antique petrol pumps which dispensed the fuel straight into vehicles, while they were parked-up on the adjacent highway. Arthur Clapham, the owner, was a decent sort of bloke and tried hard to keep my father's bills to a minimum.

On one occasion he took his van in to have the footbrake repaired and an MOT test carried out. In typical style, the footbrake pedal had failed six months earlier and he had been stopping the van with the handbrake! However, a minor accident with a bollard and a near miss involving a pedestrian on Knaresborough High Street convinced him of the error of his ways – or more likely highlighted the risk of prosecution. In addition, and perhaps more important, the van would not pass its MOT inspection with a broken footbrake.

The van was duly left at Claphams for the day to be repaired and tested. At 5pm, a slightly inebriated father went to collect the vehicle. Mr Clapham said: "I have fixed the foot pedal and that will be £17."

"What about the MOT?" enquired my father.

"Oh heck, I forgot about that," said Clapham, "Never mind. What's your registration number?"

Not surprisingly Clapham lost his MOT testing status, though for issues unrelated to father's vehicle, sometime afterwards.

Simple vehicle body repairs were often carried out by Jim Taylor, or by my father using a pop-riveter. Sadly for the family van, repair costs were often incurred at the least convenient time. A typical example of this involved an event at Ripley Castle, which should have earned father some much-needed Christmas money.

The van at that time was a Ford Thames, which had side windows, sliding doors and side seats that could be removed for transporting donkeys. The castle had decided to hold some kind of medieval pageant and father was invited to bring along two donkeys for a fee of around £8. In his haste to get there he pushed the pair of donkeys into the rather cramped vehicle and set off without inserting a couple of wooden laths designed to protect the windows. My role was to calm the donkeys and stop them scuffling around, or worse – fighting!

As you might have guessed, the donkeys did not take too kindly to their cramped accommodation. This, along with the on-going, never-ending plume of smelly smoke from father's pipe and the sea-saw movements caused by his bad driving, started to make the pair feel quite ill. Donkeys are rarely sick but many of them suffer from nerves and colic caused by stress and the rubbish they sometimes eat.

On this occasion the first donkey started swaying and broke wind, which caused the second animal to deposit the smelliest and wettest poo I have ever seen. The first then attacked the second by biting it and both started scuffling around in the back of the old van, which started to sway. Father got angry (not unusual) and started to rollick the donkeys, me and even the van. The donkeys were always nervous of father and both started to panic and back away. Suddenly there was a massive crack and the side window on the nearside broke free and fell out. Looking into the side mirror it was clear that one of the donkeys had pushed the glass free and its tail now hung out of the window.

Father was furious and let off a stream of bad language that continued unabated until we reached our destination some five miles away. After the event father was paid his £8, but the cost of using Jim Taylor for repairing the window was £9, which meant a deficit of £1. So, of course, my five shillings (25p) pocket money was forfeited for that week.

After a further window episode, father decided his donkeys should not be put in a van where they could see out, as they didn't deserve it! Actually, the real catalyst for the decision was that the van needed too much work doing to pass its MOT and so father started looking for another one. After browsing through the Knaresborough Post he saw a reconditioned van, (father's words not mine) and after a brief test-drive it was duly purchased from Pridmores Garage in Harrogate.

The van had recently been re-sprayed and looked quite smart in comparison to the normal wrecks father had owned. The fact it had a telephone number on the speedometer and filling around the bodywork

– which according to Maurice Mapplebeck had been caused by rats biting it – didn't seem to bother father.

As with all his vans, it only had a limited life span due to the tough conditions it was expected to operate under. If our vans weren't hauling donkeys around, they could be axle deep in mud in the fields or being driven around Knaresborough in second gear because father was too drunk to realise he was in the wrong gear.

The new van was a Bedford and the sliding doors on these vans (the family was to own three) always seemed to work loose over a period of time. Part of the problem was that father, who refused to wear a seat belt all his life, would leave the doors open – so that they were never properly secure.

Spring turned into summer and summer into autumn and in a short while it was dark around 4pm. My sister Katherine had always been a keen Brownie and later a Girl Guide. In those days the Girl Guides met in the parish church hall and were managed by the local women worthies. To get to the meeting and home afterwards required a walk through the churchyard, which at that time in the evening was considered too risky. One of father's watering holes was the Cross Keys public house, near the Market Place and, as always, one drink turned into four. On a Wednesday, when the pub kept longer hours for the market, father's drinking could often reach six pints – sometimes even a gallon – of beer.

Mother was always the most caring when it came to looking after the children and she told father that a pint or a gallon, she did not really care, because he was taking Katherine to Girl Guides and collecting her afterwards, and that was that. Father got into a foul mood and took Katherine off, shouting and cursing. However, things calmed down when he reached the church hall and it was agreed that he would return to collect her at 7pm.

At 6.50pm, with a face as red as a beetroot because of all the beer he had consumed earlier, he was already in position puffing and panting in the front of his van parked outside St John's Parish Church hall. He was waiting for Katherine to finish her meeting and come out. Father was never a patient person when dealing with other people (it's an Allott family trait) and on this occasion he was more stressed than normal. At around 7.05pm the Girl Guides started to come out, chatting as young people do and meeting up with their parents. Seeing Katherine sauntering towards the van, father started to make hand signals out of the window to get her to move faster.

Slightly agitated, Katherine quickly increased her speed and stopped outside the van after a few quick strides. Grabbing the sliding van door she gave it such a massive yank that it came off its runners and fell into the road.

Father flew into an absolute rage, "You stupid, silly little idiot," he began and then continued to berate and shout at her using a fountain of swear words for a further 10 minutes. Much of the rebuking took place in the presence of the other girls, the local vicar, the guides' parents and the guide leaders who were in the process of being picked up or preparing to drive off. It must have taken Katherine a lot of courage the next week to attend the guides, given the humiliating rebuke she had suffered in front of her friends.

Although I could write a complete book about the vans, my purpose in writing this specific chapter is to give readers a flavour of some of the more amusing and often embarrassing events that intertwined between father and his donkeys.

Father's vans were renowned for going wrong and, when they did, often due to lack of finance, he would usually just 'grin and bear it'. An example of this was the electric starter-motor on one of the old Bedford vans.

For more than twelve months, whenever the van needed starting, one of us would have to crawl under the vehicle to reach the ancillary starter button. While I did not mind doing this discreetly outside the house with nobody watching, it was downright embarrassing at the bottom of Knaresborough High Street with a queue of traffic behind blowing their horns and father shouting angrily out of the window for me to 'hurry up'.

On another occasion, while we were leaving the Harrogate Road field, father thought the engine was burning out and forced the van along for two miles in second gear. Great plumes of smoke came out at the sides as we travelled along, leaving father even more convinced that the engine was done for. As the van neared the old Knaresborough Hospital, he suddenly realised what the problem was and how it could easily be resolved – if he just took the handbrake off!

At about this stage in my father's life he had decided that he should have a disabled motorist's badge, as this would enable him to park outside the pubs in Knaresborough without having to walk. On one particular summer's day father decided to park outside the Groves pub, in Knaresborough Market Place. The Groves in those days was run by a delightful couple, John and Agnes Hallie. Double yellow lines had been placed down outside the pub, because of two nearby banks and also the narrowness of the road, despite it forming the main access corridor from the High Street.

He duly parked outside the Groves and went in to partake in its wares. Apparently, some bright spark decided to phone the police to tell them that they thought a bank robbery was in progress – after all these were the days of the ITV series 'The Sweeney' where the villains all used tatty vans for their robberies!

This small blue van was the last vehicle Donkey Dave owned. Due to major modifications carried out by a previous owner, it was capable of a top speed of 135 miles per hour. After father's death his gypsy friend Sharky took it away to have it crushed into a metal block.

As is still the case today, policing in Knaresborough was nearly always fairly low profile and the only person who could be mustered when the panic switch was hit, was the local female traffic warden, who was immediately sent to investigate. Father's van was well known in Knaresborough and, because he was so awkward to deal with, the police and traffic wardens ignored him for most of the time.

The local traffic warden was a tall, well-built attractive woman, called Mrs Barbara Burnham whose son, Graham had helped with the donkeys when he was younger.

She quickly identified the van as father's, but because it was on yellow lines and also due to the call from Harrogate police station (which in those days handled 999 calls) decided to give it a quick once-over to see why he had thought to park it there. In the front of the van, a clearly visible disabled badge indicated the driver was within his rights, but no such label was in the rear window. Meanwhile tipped off by a sharp-eyed pub regular, father went out to see what was happening.

"Hello Mr Allott," blustered the poor traffic warden, "I just noticed that you don't have a disabled sticker in the rear window of your van." "Oh," said father, "I used to have, but a donkey ate it."

"Oh, that's quite in order then Mr Allott," replied the warden, with a big smile as she was not sure what else she could say, and the matter was then considered closed.

Some years later he purchased a small van for carting tools and hay around. It was purchased from Jim Fulcher, an enterprising young engineer and friend of Raymond's. Jim had sometime earlier removed the van's original engine and fitted an Alfa Romeo racing engine complete with fuel injection system and a range of dials, most of which father did not understand. The van was capable of a top speed of 135 miles per hour, but was driven around Knaresborough most of the time at about 25 miles per hour!

On a small number of occasions when boy racers upset father (this was anyone under 45 with a flashy car showing off) he would let them start overtaking him and then zoom away at 90 in the inside lane. Whilst this practice was dangerous it gave father a lot of satisfaction to knock the smile off Golf GT and BMW drivers.

The family eventually nick-named this van 'the bean can,' because a hole in one wing – which I had created – had been repaired using the lid of an old bean can!

Over the years father had got into the habit of falling out with pub landlords, usually over him getting too drunk and swearing. When he became too much of a nuisance the landlord would ban him from the pub and he would have to take his custom, and the 'bean can,' elsewhere. Generally, in the later years of his life, wherever he went the 'bean can' went too. One such occasion happened when father was banned by the pubs on either side of High Bridge during the summer of 1987. So he decided to decamp to the then Royal Oak, at the bottom of Knaresborough High Street, now a private residence. Parking in the area was restricted by double yellow lines to ease the flow of heavy traffic along the A59 road. But this presented no problem to father with his disabled-driver sticker, and he parked right on a bend of the road. Two hours later with father still in the pub, a tailback of cars had built-up along the Harrogate Road with the A59 effectively reduced to a single carriageway. Not unnaturally the traffic police, concerned about the disruption, decided to investigate.

Now over a period of two hours my father could consume a large amount of beer, not to mention clocking up a lot of chat miles, and on this particular day he was making no exceptions!

The police entered the Royal Oak to enquire about the bean can and the landlord pointed the finger at father. He quickly put his pipe into his mouth to mask the smell of alcohol and obliged the police by kindly acquiescing to their request to relocate the van to the pub car park.

How father managed to avoid being arrested for drink-driving after one of his binge drinking sessions is something I shall never know. Once, when he was stopped by a police patrol vehicle and asked by the officer if he had been drinking, he replied:

"Just the one officer," said father, slurring his words.

"Is that one pint or one GALLON sir? Where do you live?"

"Just up there officer,"said father, pointing a wobbly finger in the direction of Park Crescent.

"Well I think you had better just go up there then, sir," said the officer. For once father kept very quiet and, with not so much as a splutter, did just that!

Chapter 21

Visiting Gypsies

Our father's association with gypsies was based on a fascination with their lifestyle. He particularly liked the idea that they were answerable to no-one and if things got difficult, they could just move on. Gypsies operate a loosely grouped clan system with certain of them being considered 'pure' while others, such as Irish tinkers, being considered lower down in the order. The purer gypsies would not camp near the tinkers and would sometimes go to great lengths to disassociate themselves from what they considered the lower orders. This problem still manifests itself today and is one of the reasons why, despite the fact that local authorities have been compelled to provide permanent official gypsy camps, many of the travelling fraternity will not use them.

Father learnt about the gypsies from the Hewitt family, a group of pure Romanies who had camped near Knaresborough. For reasons I am unsure of, Mrs Hewitt taught my father Romany. The language is slowly dying out and even some of the gypsies can no longer speak it. Over a period of 12 months father learnt the language, something that was to prove invaluable in the donkey-dealing business, and which on more than one occasion saved him from getting beaten up.

Mrs Hewitt had two sons and one of them, named Dolf, would sometimes call to look father up. This generally meant lots of cups of tea, a trip to the bookies and then lots of ale. At this particular time, Dolf was selling carpets house-to-house, although I thought it was particularly telling that despite the tatty state of the Park Place carpets, he never gave my parents any of his surplus wares.

The gypsies had a number of peculiar superstitions, some of which I could never fathom. For example, they would stand outside father's front door for up to an hour but would never knock. If you stepped over a bowl of crockery that was being washed up, they would break every pot and then throw the fragments away. If they drank a cup of tea they would always leave an inch in the bottom.

Gypsies have always claimed the benefit of second sight, although interestingly they can allegedly only tell the future for other people. At the age of 10 while at Topcliffe Fair, father introduced me to one of his fortune-telling friends and asked her to read my palm. Amazingly, she said I would marry someone with a name beginning with S and have two children. She went on to say that I would earn a living very differently to

Father drinks with the Gypsies, sitting outside a pub at some horse fair.

my father. All of which is true. Father was himself gifted with the benefit of second sight, but the drawback was that he nearly always had to be drunk to do it. This on some occasions caused a number of problems. These included telling people in front of their partners that their relationship would not last or telling someone a very intimate detail in front of a gaggle of friends! Fortunately father never pushed his luck at fortune telling and mostly it was a party piece that he would perform only on rare occasions.

The relationship between father and the gypsies was sometimes a marriage of convenience. He would take up some cause that generally meant mother typing various letters and, in return, the gypsies would reveal a secret or take up some task for him. A good example of this was Dolf's father. The old man technically qualified for a pension but was unable to claim it because he was always moving around. After a few letters mother and father successfully arranged for it to be paid out at a specific post office.

Some of the secrets learnt from the gypsies were to stand father in good stead with his business for the rest of his life. One of these was a secret formula to stop donkeys and horses growing white hair after they have received a cut from barbed wire. Another involved a substance called 'soup,' a foul-smelling chemical used for cleaning harnesses. Gypsies would discreetly put a dab of it on dogs, cats and horses if they

Mother & father chat to Sharky and his family at a local horse fair.

wanted them to do somersaults or, in the case of horses, rear up. From the 1960s onwards father would carry a small glass bottle of this liquid with a cork bung in it, wherever he went. A dog that kept trying to sniff his leg while he was in the pub was discreetly dabbed; the poor animal did a triple somersault before jumping out of the pub window.

A horse-riding woman who repeatedly ignored father's instructions to stay away from his donkeys was thrown by the rearing horse into a bush. A cat that urinated on father's jacket climbed up a coal-fire chimney – all were victims of 'soup.'

One of the most horrible and bizarre incidents involving gypsies came about when father purchased a tall, black female donkey from a group of shocked travellers. The most senior of them said he had to sell the donkey because his son's caravan had just burnt down. It later transpired that his son had only bought the donkey a few weeks earlier but it had brought him nothing but bad luck and he believed it to be cursed. What nobody told father was that the caravan had burnt down with the man's wife and children trapped inside it, and that they had all died!

This donkey also brought father nothing but bad luck and over the next 18-month period he broke his leg and subsequently got a thrombosis – and Leslie died. It was therefore something of a relief when the farmer who had taken the donkey for the winter telephoned to say it had just killed itself by over-eating on hen pellets. Whether the donkey deliberately committed suicide, no one will ever know.

In latter years the gypsy called Sharkey used to call to see father at Park Place. He was one of the Leeds gypsy clan and always wore an old trilby hat. He provided father with access to more donkeys and a number of purchases were made. In the typical gypsy tit-for-tat way, father repaired Sharkey's horse harness and helped him cure a sick horse.

Sharkey was like father and could drink the sea dry. Afterwards his daughter would sometimes drive him back to Leeds, as father never ever provided the gypsies with accommodation.

Gypsies would often call at Park Place when they had a problem. In the 1970s, the Dropping Well had a lady fortune teller. When the woman was not telling the future, she lived on the caravan park run by David Welch. The lady called at the house to talk to father. As the door was being opened the family dog, which had been given the nickname of an outspoken trade union leader, started barking. "Get in you bloody thing," shouted father who then addressed the dog by the trade union leader's name.

The gypsy told father she had been hallucinating and had seen the devil, so could she stay the night. "No," said father and explained that the family had no spare room. No amount of remonstrating by the gypsy would get him to change his mind and she eventually left, clearly very annoyed.

Next day, it was announced on the television that the outspoken union leader had died suddenly. Had the gypsy put a curse on the dog, and might this have been placed on the union leader because of the dog's name?

Chapter 22

Fighting for Justice

Readers will probably have gained the impression from this book that my father cared more about his donkeys than people, and to some extent this is true. However, he always had an element of compassion for those less fortunate in life and would often give tramps, dropouts and sometimes even the feeble-minded free drinks, money and nearly always sympathy.

Much of this was fuelled by a strong sense of justice. He would occasionally take on the task of arguing certain individuals' cases where he thought the authorities, especially the local council, were being over-zealous in the execution of their duties.

One such example involved an elderly old man who lived at the top of Park Row. His landlord wanted him out and started writing abusive letters about the state of the property. Father quickly intervened and dictated a large number of letters via my poor mother to the property owner. He then carried out a number of rudimentary property repairs such as rehanging the external toilet door for the old man and successfully got the landlord off the poor chap's back.

On another occasion one of his friends came to complain that he had been mugged in the toilets just behind the bus station. Father was livid that this kind of thing was going on as he felt it would be bad for business and so he decided to hang around the toilets.

A few days later he was standing next to the urinal attending to his business when the mugger decided to try his hand on father.

"If you don't want hitting or knifing old man," began the rather patronising mugger, "I would suggest you hand over your money now."

"Just a moment, while I button my fly hole up," said father – he preferred button trousers after almost having a serious accident with a zip – "And I will see what I can give you."

Sensing victory, the mugger told him to hurry up. Father always carried a walking stick that he used for directing traffic, squaring up to the odd donkey and for getting sympathy from those he wanted to influence. Occasionally it could also be whacked on the top of a bar, if father felt he was not being served promptly. Turning to the mugger who, sensing success, had relaxed, father hit him so hard with his horses-head walking stick that the young chap fell to the floor with a bang.

"Now then," said father, "How many old bastards have you mugged in here this week?"

The mugger was now in pain and things had clearly not gone the way he intended. After a further somewhat one-sided discussion, the mugger was given a big kick and then told rather dramatically by father that he had until nightfall, to leave the town. Word quickly went round Knaresborough that a vigilante was at work and the number of muggings that took place in Knaresborough during the rest of the summer fell dramatically.

Our father's sense of justice was intertwined with his association, and later friendship, with police inspector and later chief inspector Reg McCollom. Though not always on the right side of justice, father would nevertheless readily stand up to those who caused him trouble. Just such an incident happened in 1965 when three youths passed my parents' house singing and then stood shouting by the front door. Sensing a threat, and – following his bad leg and thrombosis – no longer feeling the tough fighting man he had been, he picked up the four-ten gun he kept under the bed in case of burglars. He hid it behind the inside of the front door and verbally confronted the youths outside. His main issue was that it was 10pm and the youths had caused his young son, meaning me, to wake-up. The inebriated youths, all in their twenties, started to give father some lip and one asked: "What are you going to do about it then?"

Father could stand it no more and grabbed his gun and poked it at the trio.

"I will bloody show you what I will do," he said, "I will blow your stupid heads off if you don't clear off."

A second youth said: "You won't use that, people like you are all talk!"

Now extremely angry, father loaded the gun and fired it between the youths, hitting the wall and causing clouds of dust to fly into the air. The youths suddenly became petrified statues and started mumbling: "Don't kill us please, we're sorry."

Fortunately my mother, sensing how things were progressing, had already called the police. The timely arrival of the patrol car resulted in the youths being charged with being 'drunk and disorderly' – and my father with endangering life and discharging a firearm within 50 feet of the highway.

The gun was confiscated and the matter was brought before the local magistrates. In cases like this there was always the risk that the then prosecution service would encourage the magistrates to refer the case to York for trial. Sensing the opportunity for a much bigger case, the chairman of the bench decided to cross-examine Inspector McCollom. "Was the action of Mr Allott dangerous?" he asked – in an attempt to lead the witness!

My father's sense of justice was intertwined with his association, and later friendship, with Reg McCollom. The man on the left is Reg McCollom. Also featured is the local police sergeant, his horse and local children.

"No," said Inspector McCollom. "Men like Mr Allott are from the farming community and they are born with guns in their arms."

Somewhat angry that this could not be blown into a bigger case, the magistrates fined my father 50 shillings (£2.50) for firing his gun within fifty feet of the Queen's highway and ordered the police to return the gun. Most people would have been delighted with the outcome, as even in those days a custodial sentence would have been a clear distinct possibility. In contrast my father was totally incensed at the outcome and returned home from the Knaresborough Court House in a foul mood. He believed that the real guilty people had been the youths and he had simply been defending his home. After all, he had told the Bench: "An Englishman's home is his castle!"

His solution was to heat a plate until it was almost red hot, with the intention of dropping it into the lap of the magistrates' chairman with the words: "Have a hot sentence yourself sir." But, as on many of these occasions, quick thinking by mother talked him out of it, and the plate was taken off the cooker's hot ring and allowed to burn a mark at the side of the sink!

One of father's shortcomings was that he suffered from paranoia involving all sorts of perceived threats. The first problem I can remember involved one of our neighbours, Mr Fall, who owned a nearby local shop that fronted onto the High Street and backed onto Park Place. The problem arose over a dispute concerning the narrow dirt track at the front of 8 Park Place. Mr Fall, who lived just two properties away, and had the local dairy, took it upon himself to regularly drive past my parents' house and in the process one day knocked into Leslie's pram. Both mother and father were absolutely furious and felt violated. My father swiftly made the decision to close off car access to the road in front of their house, by installing a large wooden post into the middle of the road.

This was followed by father sealing it into the ground with concrete and Mr Fall lifting it out. Each removal resulted in a bigger hole and even more wedging. The whole situation deteriorated with my father and a neighbour, Joe Kirk, verbally putting Mr Fall right. Various insults and solicitors' letters changed hands and eventually an uneasy peace came about with father, not for the first or last time, getting his own way.

Various other incidents happened with neighbours at Park Place and while I don't intend to recall them all, a less serious and more amusing event occurred around a year later. It was about 8pm and I was having difficulty sleeping.

Mother came to enquire what was wrong and I told her that the house walls were moving in. The real reason for my lack of sleep was that Malcolm, who lived next door with his mother, had decided to do some unplanned renovating.

Malcolm, who was then in the prime of his life, worked during the day as a plumber and in an evening was involved it would seem in a series of failed home improvements. Number 6 Park Place adjoined our home and over the space of just two years, Malcolm had removed a substantial amount of plaster, wood and bricks. As time progressed, my parents became increasingly concerned as nothing ever seemed to be put back to replace the materials that had been taken away.

The fact that Malcolm had broken my sleep pattern was the last straw for my parents, and father decided to shout through the wall in order to get him to stop banging.

Malcolm started shouting at father and apparently 'gave him a lot of lip'. However, father was not a man to be trifled with so round he went to hammer on the door, threatening Malcolm with dire consequences when he found him. His mother answered the door and she said that Malcolm had been under a lot of pressure at work. Father said he would be under even more pressure when his fist hit him and matters were left at that. A few days later, it transpired that Malcolm's mother had confided in another neighbour, that Malcolm had become so afraid as to what Mr Allott would do to him, that he had allegedly hidden under his mother's bed!

In the early 1970s care in the community was undergoing one of its reorganisation phases, and as a result a number of harmless but eccentric people were released from hospital – one being Ernest Crowe. He had lived in Knaresborough for years and had worked with father at the local auction. He subsequently suffered some kind of trauma, which resulted in him being sent to Whixley, a nearby mental hospital.

The untimely closure of the hospital resulted in Crowe being discharged into the community and ultimately led to him sleeping rough on the streets of Knaresborough. Chief Inspector McCollom had the town patrolled with military precision and had a public inspection of his officers every Thursday evening, in the Market Place. A semi-vagrant sleeping on Knaresborough's streets was unthinkable and McCollom wanted him transferring to another institution. However, every time his officers tried to talk to Crowe, he ran off. To make matters worse he could not be arrested because he was not classified as severely mentally ill and therefore apart from sleeping rough had done nothing wrong.

To resolve the matter, McCollom engaged father to deal with the problem. Despite his gruff exterior, father was always decent with those for whom he felt sorry. Within a matter of hours, Crowe had been found and was sitting in my parents' living room. Mother made him a hot meal and father gave him a shave. Half-decent clothes were found for him and within a few hours he looked quite presentable. The next day my father took him on the bus to York and left him at Clifton, a hospital which took in the mentally ill on a voluntary basis.

McCollom was very grateful to my father and wrote him a nice letter outlining how public spirited he had been. The Crowe event was to prove very useful when a serious incident arose at Bilton Fields.

My father always tried to manage Bilton Fields as though it was his own property. The fact that he simply had a donkey-riding concession from the council, which he was required to pay for and get renewed every few years, was an irrelevance to him. During the summer, youths riding bikes past the donkeys would be asked to dismount and it was common for cheeky kids to be clouted by father or, in extreme cases, to have their bikes thrown in the river. Most kids in Knaresborough knew what was likely to happen and were generally polite where father was concerned. Equally, people obstructing the path of the donkeys would be asked to move and courting couples on the grass would sometimes be asked to find somewhere more discreet, for fear that they might upset father's beloved donkeys!

In the early 1970s two men in their twenties came down to the donkeys and told my father that his animals used to give longer rides and they could remember them previously having walked into the adjoining field. This was quite a dangerous comment to make and father quickly told them where to get off. One of the men – the biggest – then started telling father off for swearing in front of the kids who were helping with the donkeys. Looking back, it seems the men had decided to deliberately provoke a fight with father although, to this day, their motive remains very unclear.

Heated exchanges continued and as tempers flared, the biggest man lunged at my father. He saw him coming, spun round, and threw him to the floor in front of the donkeys. Within a matter of seconds, father then got the first man in a headlock and pushed his thumb into his face. What people passing must have thought, I have no idea! Despite my father's much senior age he got the better of the biggest man and the second man started to panic and tried to break the fight up.

I quickly ran to a phone box located at the corner of the High Bridge adjacent to the Worlds End Pub and dialled 999 to get the police. On my return father agreed to let the first man, who now had blood dripping from his face, go providing he agreed to behave himself! The man realised he had no choice and he willingly confirmed. The injured man on getting up praised my father's strength, before both would-be assailants headed quickly out of the fields and to the bus stop on the other side of the road from Bilton Fields.

Shortly afterwards a police car arrived and, accompanied by father with its blue light flashing, it sped off in the direction of Harrogate after the bus, which the men had recently boarded. The bus was stopped on Harrogate Road and the two men were arrested, put into the police car and taken back to Knaresborough for questioning.

Naturally, my father's sense of outrage and his quest for justice again put him at odds with McCollom and the law. Father wanted them charged, beaten-up and then banged up, but McCollom had other concerns.

The men were placed in cells at the police station to cool off. A medical examination of the first man revealed a much-marked face, due to father's thumb action. McCollom eventually let the men out of the cells in return for a promise not to take any legal action against father.

McCollom was concerned that the first man would have a big scar and it would seem he felt a little sorry for him. However, father did not feel the same way and was angry that McCollom would not let him visit them in the cells with a police truncheon – so that he could dish out his own justice!

After a period of reflection, father saw McCollom's point and the trade-off between the two men continued until the chief inspector's retirement a few years later. A less serious and funnier incident that brought the two together again, was the 'Riverside Flasher'. Apparently a middle-aged woman had been flashed at and the police arrived in Bilton Fields in great numbers. Father agreed to help them track the man across the fields and adjoining paths and this ultimately ended in the man's arrest. What the flasher must have thought when father told him in all seriousness that he had seen a bigger penis on a dog, I shudder to imagine!

The flashing event got father back in the good books with McCollom and the other officers at Knaresborough police station, and he subsequently received yet another letter of thanks for being so public-spirited, this time from the Chief Constable. However, even father could sometimes push his luck too far and one such event still sits vividly in my mind. In the 1960s father nearly always went to the library on a Thursday evening. In those days nearly all the shops in Knaresborough closed for half a day on Thursday afternoons, but the library stayed open into the evening. Ironically, today the library now closes early on a Thursday whilst most of the shops stay open!

To reassure residents, the police used to hold a Thursday evening parade in the Market Place. The parade was managed by Inspector McCollom who, as part of a local public relations exercise, inspected the officers, before despatching them off to their respective community beats. Coincidentally the police parade happened at the same time that father was striding across the marketplace to reach the library. Normally, father would not have given the parade a passing glance but on this occasion he had been drinking earlier and therefore decided to inspect the local Bobbies himself.

One officer was told he had dirty shoes another officer was accused of spilling food on his tunic, whilst another was told he had a dirty whistle. To start with, the police took it all in good fun. But as father continued rambling on, McCollom said that if father did not depart he would have no choice but to charge him with obstructing an officer in the execution of his duty. Fortunately, he took the blunt hint and walked off to hassle the poor library staff!

One of the issues that wound father up the most during his residence at Park Place concerned the social club, which was located opposite our home. Father hated the club and blamed it for providing beer for a whole gang of low-lifes, who he accused of lowering the tone of the neighbourhood!

Various confrontations and rows took place with those who parked at the top of Park Crescent to frequent the club. This ultimately resulted in father claiming a yard of public highway adjacent to the wall in order to maintain it. Harrogate Borough Council, which by now was responsible for local government in Knaresborough, should have resolved the matter. However, the authority was always nervous of dealing with father – with good reason – and therefore chose not to intervene.

As readers can imagine, forcing motorists to park a yard away from the wall went down very badly with locals, especially when father told them to move. To inflame tensions even more a 'Keep Clear' board and cones were often put out by father on the days when the club organised trips and special events. When one of the club people deliberately parked on the board and asked father what he was going to do he received the response that he would ram his old banger into the questioner's new car! Needless to say, the car was quickly moved.

On another occasion he went to shout at someone parking while he was shaving and covered in foam. I subsequently overhead the recipient of father's tongue-lashing telling his pal that he had just been given a rollicking by a mad man who was foaming at the mouth.

One or two of the people who frequented the club really tried father's patience and they were the ones earmarked by him for some very special treatment. One woman, whose husband drove a clapped-out old car, was overheard saying to other drinkers, that the club would be allowed to stay open until midnight because her husband was the chief of police.

After the couple had gone into the club and it had become very dark, father got out an old rope and tied it to the back of the car's bumper and the adjacent concrete street light. At around 11.30pm the pair could be heard returning to their car, still shouting and carrying on because they had been refused a further drink. After some kafuffle, the couple finally got into their car and started revving the engine just to annoy father. Suddenly the man let his clutch out and there was one almighty bang, as the rear bumper bar detached itself from his car. Right on cue, father dialled 999 and told the police that two drunks were trying to steal a lamp-post. A fast police response and a night in the cells can do wonders for the most annoying people and neither of them was ever seen again on Park Place. This became a 'win-win' situation for father because he got yet another letter of commendation from the police!

As the years rolled by, father got more ambitious with his actions to reap revenge on the Park Place Social Club members. In November 1988 this led to him nailing a large board to the side of his house. In big white scruffy letters the board read: "The 'hole in the wall' will be closed for essential repairs on December the 25th".

Slowly the weeks rolled by and everyone in the town became very interested as to what would happen. In early December, Harrogate Council wrote to father, asking him not to close the wall permanently. Local Park Place Social Club members started to grumble whenever they saw the sign.

On Christmas Day father got up at 6am rather excitedly and nailed the wall up using large pieces of timber, which meant that motorists parking on Park Crescent and intent on visiting the club had to jump the wall. At around 11.50am a large number of people gathered at the blocked hole and started shouting towards my parents' house. The police were called and a large blue van arrived with a number of officers. Club members were threatened with being charged with a breach of the peace and were told to disperse. Eventually after some arguing with the police, who were not amused, and further provocation by the crowd after which the police threatened to make arrests, the group broke up and went their separate ways.

At about 12.30pm my Christmas lunch was disrupted for a short while when father phoned in a panic. "Philip, Philip, you've got to come up quickly as there are some people I want you to help me hit!" As the then district councillor for the Knaresborough East Ward and a former town Mayor, I clearly had no intention of getting involved in a brawl and so made a polite excuse about my lunch going cold and promised to come as soon as possible.

Later, on arriving at my parents' house about 3.30pm for Christmas tea, my Auntie Mary, (also see chapter 24) who had begun going to my parents every Christmas Day for lunch following grandfather's death, said it had been a most frightening experience. Mary said that in future she would be having her Christmas lunch with members of the Collins Court Residents Association because it would be less stressful.

In contrast father said it had been one of the most exciting Christmases he had even known – and he vowed to close the 'hole in the wall' the following year.

Chapter 23

Other Donkey Owners

As time progressed, father's name and reputation spread around and there was a constant trickle of requests for help from other donkey owners in the locality. He would often be called in to examine sick donkeys, to trim their hooves or simply to provide general advice on care and maintenance of the animals.

Unfortunately for me, the one who generally acted as his assistant on these forays, most of the events seemed to take place after school and few of them were uneventful. One particular trip was to the charming village of Burton Leonard, which lies between Harrogate and Ripon. Living in the village at the time was a man who was lodging at a house and looking after their donkeys while the owners were on holiday.

This may have been an unusual set of circumstances, because as a rule it was the owners who would contact father when they needed his expertise. But the call when it came was all too familiar; the donkeys were not doing too well and were not eating properly. The house-sitter was more than a little concerned for the donkeys' welfare. We duly set off for Burton Leonard in one of father's vans which, on this occasion, had a sober driver.

We found the donkeys were living in a small paddock that was not big enough for their needs. Frankly, it had been over-grazed so all that was left for the donkeys to eat were bits of what could best be described as second-class pasture.

Father prescribed a move to some fresh pasture and suggested an evening feed of oats. And as was generally the custom on these visits his suggestion of trimming the animals' hooves was accepted and he and I began a task which father always knew would earn him an extra few quid for his visit – as well as allowing him to demonstrate his skills as a farrier, while I was merely left to hold the hoof.

For reasons explained in an earlier chapter, the Knaresborough donkeys all behaved themselves when their hooves were being cut. However, 'guest' donkeys obviously had no experience of father's management skills and were therefore prone to playing up.

On this occasion, one of the pair of donkeys on the holding was tied to the pole of a carport which had a low privet hedge adjoining it. The lodger went inside to make us some coffee while father and I attended to the hooves of the bigger of the two donkeys. While the coffee was being prepared the donkey became a bit frisky, pushed me aside and knocked father over the hedge. He of course, was not best amused and the donkey got such a cursing that it began to cower in a corner.

Father waved his rasp at it and told it straight that if there was any more misbehaving it would get some 'treatment' with the tool. The donkey's hoof was then picked up again and work continued on the cutting without further alarms and with a totally compliant donkey. The lodger was somewhat amazed when he returned with the coffee to find the donkey standing well-behaved – and when it looked as if it might do otherwise, father waved his rasp around.

The lodger then let slip the fact that the local vet had flatly refused to cut the donkey's hooves any more after an embarrassing incident similar to the one with the privet hedge – but pricklier, as the vet had been deposited in a rose bush.

Most of our visits included some kind of incident and not all of them involved donkeys, because on more than a few occasions we did not reach our destination before being involved in controversy. I can recall one day setting off for Follifoot, a village only a few miles from Knaresborough, to visit one particular donkey.

However, we did not get too far on this occasion. After crossing Low Bridge as we left the town to head up Bland's Hill, our van suddenly crossed the centre white line – and hit a Morris Minor driven by a man wearing a pork-pie hat who was promptly accused by father of not being able to drive properly.

This not unnaturally brought a fierce protest from beneath the hat, to the effect that the man had moved left as far as he could, even to the point of the Morris's nearside wheels dragging against the kerb, but the van had still managed to hit him.

A heated discussion took place before it was eventually agreed that father's insurance company would resolve the matter. The journey then continued to Follifoot where the donkey we had been called out to see had its hooves trimmed. Some years later this particular donkey was purchased by father and given the Riverside name of Leo.

At least on this occasion we did, eventually, reach our destination. There were other times when we did not, with one memorable trip seeing us beating a hasty retreat after yet another road accident. Father had set off on this particular trip in a state of high excitement as the call for help had come from one of no fewer than three breweries, which provide major sources of employment in the North Yorkshire market town of Tadcaster. Father, as usual, went into care mode, though this time the air of authority he used to respond to the phone call was tinged with expectations of what 'benefits' might lie at the trip's end. Although the SOS from the brewery's finance director was for help with a rebellious donkey, that was not the thought uppermost in father's mind as we set off. Any possible problems were outweighed by the vision of sampling the wares of the nearby brewery!

Again the time of departure was after school and father had decided to 'prepare' himself in advance for the anticipated free drinks by downing a few in Knaresborough. As was usually the way with father, this preparation took priority over getting the tools ready for checking donkeys' hooves.

In those days – and this was a rare occurrence – father had not a van but a car, an elderly Morris Oxford. It was a vehicle that had already been the subject of police chastisement earlier in the year. Inspector McCollom had told father off for keeping hay in the boot, as he believed it could easily ignite.

This was not an unreasonable assumption for a car which, having been acquired from one of my uncles, was already nearly worn-out and prone to regular backfiring. But the possibility of hay igniting was nothing compared to what was to occur on the relatively short trip from Knaresborough to Tadcaster a few months later.

When I got home from school on the day in question, it was to be greeted by father, waiting on the doorstep, in a state of high excitement. "Come on lad, come on lad, there's work to be done," was the only bit of explanation I received. I quickly changed from my school uniform into tatty work clothes and we set off in the direction of Tadcaster, a well known northern brewery town.

Father never liked travelling on dual-carriageway roads such as the A1. To him a scenic route was always preferable, particularly one without traffic lights – so we meandered along at a steady 30mph in a car which was of course capable of far higher speeds.

Father, with his pipe in his mouth, chatted away on the journey about people and places long gone. Tadcaster in those days was one of those towns where the main road still cut right through the centre and where there were vehicles parked all the way along. This tended to obscure entrances to properties and as we progressed down the street trying to locate our destination, father became more and more frustrated and began to curse, at the same time twisting his head to peer behind him out of the windows, fearing he had missed the brewery house. We knew this was on our left, but before locating our destination there was an almighty bang as the Morris Oxford collided with a stationary VW Beetle, ripping off its running board and shearing its wing.

"Bloody hell," was father's initial outcry, swiftly followed by: "Hold on to your hat lad, hold on to your hat," as we left Tadcaster at a speed considerably quicker than we had journeyed to it.

By the time we reached Boston Spa, the speedometer needle was touching 80, and that in what is now – and no doubt was then – a 30mph area.

He stopped the car to inspect the damage. Cars like the Morris Oxford were built by craftspeople and were vehicles their owners could be proud of. They were built to last from the best materials, so the damage to the Morris was limited to one small piece of panelling adjacent to a wheel arch.

However, to father this spelled trouble – of the legal kind. The rest of the journey home was made without comment as he puzzled over what to say to the police when – inevitably, he felt – they came calling. By the end of the journey he had his story worked out. It went like this: Joy-riders from the despised Park Place Social Club had stolen the vehicle and banged it into a wall before returning it in its damaged state.

Sure enough three days later police, alerted by a passer-by in Tadcaster, arrived to question father. Although he was charged with careless driving, he stuck to his story and the lack of corroborative evidence meant that the case never went to court. The Tadcaster donkey never did receive father's attention – and he never got his free beers.

Chapter 24

Buying the Land at Knaresborough

Father was very proud of the Harrogate Road land and would sometimes bore to tears visitors who might innocently ask the odd question about the hedge or trees. As mentioned briefly in chapter 12, when he had taken over the land as a tenant in the 1960s, the land agents Jackson-Stops & Staff had assigned the lease to father and his heirs and successors. This, in effect, meant that the business could continue in perpetuity and this greatly appealed to him because at times he could become really obsessed over his own mortality.

In 1974 an out-of-the-blue letter arrived from the agents informing father that the land was to be sold by public auction later that year. Three parcels of land were involved, one on each side of Harrogate Road and the third down Bilton Fields, next to Foolish Wood. As can be imagined, father was horrified and saw all his future business plans evaporating almost overnight. According to father, there were rumours circulating the town at the time that there were three potential buyers for the land: The Dropping Well Estate, David Welch and an unknown person.

Mrs MacLean has subsequently informed me that the Dropping Well Estate never intended to purchase the land, but obviously if it had, it would have extended the Estate and given it the option of combining it with the caravan site and making a bigger park. David Welch wanted to buy the land because it would allow him to link up with a section he owned between father's land and the Harrogate Golf Club. Moreover, it would also reduce his dependency on renting land from the Dropping Well Estate. As was typical in my parents' household, father ranted and raved while mother tried to think of a way out. The last thing either of them wanted was a tenancy with the Dropping Well Estate or Mr Welch.

The first port of call was to the Midland Bank (now HSBC) to see if the money could be borrowed to purchase the land. Given the volatile nature of the donkey business and the various overdrafts my parents had run over the years, the manager was not too keen. However, the family did have some employment security because mother had recently taken a job working for a financial investment company, MacLean Associates, owned by Ian MacLean, Shirley MacLean's husband at that time.

The bank manger therefore considered the matter for a few days. After also consulting head office he agreed to lend the family the estimated £3,000 needed to purchase the land. However, this required my

Derek Tucker gives Gerry his favourite tipple, a cup of tea, whilst the author writes a racing performance card.

parents to put up the family home as security and to accept crippling, double-digit interest rate charges. Clearly the situation was virtually a non-starter for my parents, as merely meeting the interest payments was potentially going to be a major problem.

On November the 29th, MacLean Associates decided to make mother redundant and gave her just a calendar month's notice. This was clearly a crashing blow as the sale was due to take place on the 19th of December. With only a few weeks to go before the sale my parents' position regarding borrowing money to buy the land was now virtually a non-starter. On paper at least my parents' chances of buying the land at this stage were virtually nil. However, as is so often the case, with careful planning and good tactics, victory can be snatched from the jaws of defeat.

Mother quickly dusted her CV down and started applying for jobs. Within a matter of weeks she had secured a new position working as a secretary for what was then the Harrogate College of Further Education. However, this still did not solve the problem of borrowing the money for the land at a sensible interest rate.

Help came from an unexpected quarter and my parents were always to be very grateful. In 1971 grandfather Allott had died after a short illness and left a widow, his second wife Mary Allott. Mary had married Cyril in June 1970 and was a quiet, retiring type, very different to the noisy and sometimes boisterous Allotts. When grandfather had been alive he had kept Allott family contact with Mary to a minimum. So over the next two years, the family got to know Mary much better and she even once went on holiday with us – but only once!

When Mary heard of our parents' plight she kindly agreed to provide them with the extra money to buy the Harrogate Road fields.

Grandfather had left £2,000 in his will and the interest was to be paid to Mary for life and his children (David and Margaret) were to receive the lump sum on her death. However, Mary very generously made the £1,000, partly generated from the sale of grandfather's car, immediately available to father. She also agreed to lend the remainder of the money at a very low interest rate. Were it not for Mary's generous nature the land on Harrogate Road would not now be in the Allott family's ownership.

Meanwhile, father made contact with the MacIntosh family to ask, as a sitting tenant, for some kind of preference or even a private sale. Discussions took place and it was agreed that although the auction would have to go ahead the auctioneer would try and bang down his gavel when the land had made its reserve price of £3,000, although clearly no guarantee could be given.

The auction took place at the George Hotel with both blind bidding and open bidding. According to mother and father, people present were absolutely amazed to see father bidding and even more surprised when he outbid another buyer and the gavel quickly went down at £3,000. My parents were elated and could not believe their luck. Father was so excited that he could not sleep for four weeks and ended up having to take some cough medicine in the evenings, which had the side-effect of inducing drowsiness.

Meanwhile the manager at the Midland Bank was furious when, because of a banking error, he thought father had written out a cheque without the necessary funds. Whilst mother was at work, he phoned father to chastise him and to tell him that the cheque could not be honoured. Sure of his ground, father for once bit his tongue and told the manager to check for money that had been paid in.

Thirty minutes later the phone rang again. "Hello Mr Allott, I do most sincerely apologise, it would seem that there has been some kind of banking error.

"I have now found the money you have paid in and of course your account is fully in order. If you need to borrow any money for building on your new land or anything else please don't hesitate to ask me. Once again many apologies." So spoke the rather panicky manager!

"Thank you very much and I have no doubt we'll be in touch," said father, who behaved very graciously – at least on this occasion.

Owning the land was a big boost to my parents' self-confidence and they walked tall for a change. Mary told them that now they were landowners father should start dressing smarter, but this was definitely a step too far for him.

Around 1988 father decided to apply for planning permission to build a modest bungalow on the land. Local planning permission is granted by Harrogate Borough Council and, after due consideration, members of the committee came down to inspect the land. Father explained that all he wanted to do was to live with his donkeys and look after them, but the committee members were having none of it. The councillors decided that he should not be given permission and it was refused sometime later. Mother and father were very upset and I personally felt that the council had been less than sympathetic.

Sadly, father and mother never lived to see their bungalow and it would seem once again that the dreaded Harrogate Borough Council had got the better of them!

Chapter 25

Earning an Honest Living

During the 1970s the family's expenses continued to rise and as mentioned in the previous chapter mum had to work full-time. From the early 1970s onwards, she worked as a secretary for a number of businesses and eminent organisations including Harrogate College, the clerk to the magistrates' court and, lastly, the Community Health Council.

Father disliked the idea of mother having to work, but given the poor capacity of his donkey business to generate a lot of cash for a growing family, he did not have a lot of choice. After some debate he decided to go chimney sweeping again.

New chimney sweeping rods were purchased from a firm in Leeds and an advert was then placed in the local paper. The work came in fits and starts, with father writing each phone booking slowly in his book.

After sweeping on a Wednesday father would often visit the Groves Hotel in the evening without changing. Being covered from top to toe in black soot did not seem to bother him. Father had his own place at the bar, where he could stand with a single black finger touching the counter. Chimney sweeping is a dry, dirty business and after a heavy sweeping session, his appetite for beer could be very severe. After eight or nine pints and somewhat inebriated he would go home.

At around this time I obtained a small pocket recording device and decided to push my luck. I pre-recorded, in a very squeaky voice, a call from a Mr Chiwi to father on the pretext that he wanted his chimney sweeping. Gaps were left in the recording for father to answer and after a few practices I went off to make the call at the phone box, located at the time in Knaresborough Bus Station. Raymond in the meantime listened against the front room door to hear how father would answer.

The call started OK with father saying in his patronising semi-drunk way: "Hello, hello, sweep here, just a moment, just a moment let me get my book." Unfortunately I had not left sufficient of a gap in the recording and the tape therefore continued on: "Can you come on Tuesday, my address is Abbey Road ..." "Just a moment, just a moment," blustered father, "... Knaresborough, North Yorkshire," the pre-recorded tape continued.

"Well stuff you if you're not going to listen," barked father before slamming the phone down.

Knowing that my cover could be blown at any minute I quickly

David the chimney sweep, dressed up for a wedding

rushed the two-minute distance back home. Meanwhile at Park Place, Raymond, unable to contain himself further, had started to laugh. Just as I arrived home I saw father, who had now realised that he had been set up, reward Raymond with an almighty smack. "How dare you pretend to be a foreigner, you naughty little twat," said father. The more Raymond protested, the more father rollicked him. In the living room next door, Katherine and I nearly burst ourselves laughing.

As a business spin-off he would also make himself available for hire at local weddings. Dressed in his chimney sweep outfit complete with brushes he looked quite a comical figure and would stand next to the bride and groom to wish them luck. This proved quite a lucrative winter sideline for father. At many of the weddings not only would the happy couple pay him an attendance fee, but they would also tip him quite handsomely, on the basis that this would bring them good luck. In addition, he loved being the centre of attention. All went well for a number of months.

As time went by father became more confident in his new money generating role and in the past this is when things started to go wrong. Arriving rather early for one particular afternoon wedding at

Knaresborough Parish Church, he decided to retire to the local pub to wait. Inside the pub, he soon struck a discussion with a number of the locals about his donkeys and within the space of an hour he had (as usual) consumed quite a large amount of beer. Suddenly realising that he still had the wedding to attend, he made his excuses and scurried off back to the local church.

By now the church service was in full swing and father stood in the doorway waiting for the organ to strike up toccata, so that he could be the first person outside to greet the happy couple. On cue the organ started and within a matter of minutes the church doors burst open, whilst the church bells in the background rang out wedding chimes. However, the happy couple who came out was not the man and woman who had booked father. After about a minute, it dawned on him that he was at the wrong wedding!

However, the happy couple were delighted to see father and wrongly assumed that one of their relatives had booked him. Meanwhile, back at Park Place mother was having a telephone conversation with a very distressed groom, who was demanding his money back plus compensation for breach of contract.

I was not privy to what mother said to father when he somewhat belatedly returned home, but what I do know is that his enthusiasm for attending weddings evaporated and he attended very few after this unfortunate incident!

Over a period of a few years father's revived sweeping business started to build momentum. These activities were not missed by the always vigilant Inland Revenue which, after some preliminary enquires, decided it was time to invite him for an interview.

Father, a master at playing the authorities at their own game, prepared carefully in advance and selected the dirtiest most ripped clothing he could find. In the local district in the 1970s the tax office was based in some high-rise offices, called Copthall Towers near Harrogate railway station.

On arrival, he was taken from reception into a smart private office. It was at this point that he started knocking off the donkey muck he had deliberately brought in on his boots. The young tax officer ignored his shuffling and started to ask some questions. "Just a moment," said father who then raised his arm and gave its pit a great scratch. "Sorry about that, I think it's something I caught last week while sweeping an old house."

The young tax officer began to panic and now seemed intent on cutting the interview short. "If you could just keep a book of the work you do and let us have a list each year, which will be all right," he blustered.

Sensing victory, father said: "I don't make a lot of money with the business because of the difficulty in bending my bad leg. This coupled with my infected ankle really causes me a lot of jip. Would you like to see my bad ankle?" he enquired.

"No, no Mr Allott," began the tax officer. "We are very busy people, please try and keep a list of the jobs you have done and how much you earn each year. Now if you will excuse me, I must get on."

"Are you sure you don't need anything else?" asked father.

However the office door was now opened and the tax officer was already shooing father, at arm's length, in the direction of the lift with the parting shot of: "Goodbye Mr Allott."

Father never did keep proper revenue records, although it is unlikely after taking account of operating costs that he made enough to pay tax anyway.

Officialdom and father never really got on, as readers of the book will probably have gathered. One rather amusing incident related to this came when father needed a visitor's passport. In the pre-Lockerbie days, UK subjects could get a temporary passport from any Crown Post Office. This required a trip to Harrogate and having by then reached driving age, I agreed to take father along. The passport required two small photos, which could be obtained from a booth located at the back of the Post Office. Father duly climbed into the booth and sat patiently waiting for the machine to operate. After a few minutes of inaction he looked away, just at the point when the flash went off. When the pictures came out he was not looking at the camera and his expression appeared distinctly dodgy. "Sorry sir," said the brusque lady behind the counter, "I am not passing this application, as you are not looking at the camera."

"Well stuff you," said father to the lady, "You can stick your holiday because I'm not going anyway!"

What the women must have thought I can only speculate. It took me 20 minutes to calm father down and get him to have some more pictures taken. "I'll pass that, you look rather nice there," said another of the counter staff when she saw the new pictures. "I don't really want to go on holiday," retorted father.

"He's very excited about his holiday," I stammered.

"You can say that again," said the second lady behind the counter, as she gave father a childlike grin.

Chapter 26

Farming

When he started Starbeck School, father became friendly with Alan Dunn, or 'Dunny' as he was more affectionately known. Alan's father farmed the land next door to the Todd's acreage and when his father passed away, Alan inherited the farm. Alan's farming forte was machinery while father's was animals, so the two of them would often pool their skills and work together at peak times.

Until the 1970s Alan's farm was a mixture of arable crops and livestock, which used to be very typical of the North Yorkshire area. During the 1960s Dunny sold part of his land to a charitable trust, Henshaw's Society for Blind People, which runs a residential college for partially sighted youngsters adjacent to the Bogs Lane land father rented. A few years later, when the trust was flush with cash, it purchased the Todd land and father became its tenant.

Unlike father, Dunny, who was the landowner, had benefited from the sale and had been able to invest the capital generated elsewhere in his remaining farmland. The lend/help agreement between father and Dunny continued to work extremely well. Through Alan, father gained access to tractors, bailers and other equipment that would not have been viable if he had had to buy them all.

In addition, father's Bogs Lane land also backed onto Dunny's and this made it easier to gain tractor access for tillaging and haymaking. For over thirty years father would meadow the Bogs Lane land during the summer, in order to provide a hay crop for feeding the stay-at-home donkeys during the winter months.

The hay was nearly always cut and bailed during the week of the Great Yorkshire Show. Haymaking was a tough pastime which required the bales to be collected from the bailer and loaded onto trailers for transporting to Knaresborough for storage.

In the later years up to 300 bales could be made at Bogs Lane in just a matter of a few hours. The labour logistics involved required father to find some temporary staff.

Frankly some of the people who came to help, like Ribena-man, were well past their prime. Ribena-man earned his nickname because, after lifting about ten bales, he would go red in the face and would look as if he was going to pass-out. Other people roped-in to help included some of

Left to right are Alan Dunn, Steven Dunn and Alan's grandson. Note the poor condition of the nearest tractor. Alan's engineering skills have kept machinery like this running for many years.

the bigger donkey helpers and even a few pensioners such as the appropriately named Jack Bailes.

Most of the buildings at Bogs Lane were dilapidated and, after baling, the majority of the hay would be loaded onto trailers for bringing down to Knaresborough. Many of these trailers were not roadworthy and the tractors that were required to tow them were even less so. On one occasion, Raymond was driving a tractor and trailer on Bogs Lane and hit a car's wing mirror. The driver phoned the police and not long afterwards Raymond found himself briefly detained in a police cell. Apparently Dunny, so afraid that he would be prosecuted for having an unroadworthy vehicle, had told the police when questioned, that Raymond had stolen it. Fortunately the timely intervention of father resulted in the record being put straight and in the police releasing brother Raymond uncharged.

In return for haymaking help father would try and help Dunny with his calves or with other less glamorous jobs, such as rat catching or moving sacks around. Two or three trips to Knaresborough would be required by a tractor and trailer, with each bale being manually loaded and then unloaded on arrival. Much of the hay was stored in a large Dutch barn which father had constructed in the mid-1960s.

Farming of the land in Knaresborough was basic and consisted of harrowing in spring and winter plus some tillaging. This, together with shed and fence repairs, was just about the sum total of the farm work. In the early days of the Knaresborough fields a great deal of work had been put into finding a number of the soiled land drains. To find these, father had used a pair of copper rods which worked on the principle that when the rods crossed the drainpipe was directly below.

Large weeds and brambles were left to the donkeys to demolish. For the first two months after the donkeys moved into the Harrogate Road field, they were not seen. Over time the donkeys slowly but surely moved around the field eating up thistles, nettles and, in fact, almost everything that was there.

The land at Harrogate Road in the early days of its leasing was boggy and father made things worse for himself by parking inside the first field. Originally he had parked on Harrogate Road, but a parking ticket quickly showed him the error of his ways and he therefore decided to park in the field. On returning to the van on this occasion, after it had been left for a few hours, it had sunk to its axles. It took us two hours to lift it out, using ramps and a hydraulic jack.

However, father continued to park the van in the fields during the summer months and this point was not lost on the donkeys, who also noticed the sandwiches which mother prepared and packed-up for the helpers to eat during their meal-break. In a daring raid, Sooty, one of the more intelligent donkeys, pulled back the side-opening van door with his teeth and ate all the young helpers' sandwiches. What father threatened to do to the donkey cannot be repeated here but fortunately, apart from the good cursing, the naughty animal got off scot-free.

Once or twice a year Dunny would come down and cut the front hedge. This continued until the 1970s when he began contracting out the work, but he continued to provide tractors and haymaking support for father and then mother until they both died. If there are to be any awards for the unsung heroes of this book, Alan Dunn must be a serious contender.

Chapter 27

Droving

One day in the early 1970s there was a knock at front door. "Who the heck is that?" muttered father, as he went to open the door. Standing there was the manager, from Thornton and Linley (see chapter three). He explained to father that the livestock auction which took place every Monday at the back of the Borough Bailiff pub on the High Street, was desperately short of staff again. Would father come and help?

Father had given up cattle droving after he broke his leg and in addition he was also still annoyed at Thornton and Linley for putting a hundred pounds on the selling price of the house he bought way back in 1963! After some discussion, all conducted on the front door step, it was agreed that father would go in to help on the Monday for a fee of around £3 per hour. Typically, this would generate around £15, which was not unreasonable, given that the contents would all go into his back pocket for beer and splitting with mother later.

Work at the auction started at around 10.30am with animals arriving from farms in the surrounding area. The main auction lots were pigs, sheep and cattle and it was normal practice at that time to sell the smaller stock first. On the arrival of pigs, father was expected to show them into various metal pens located under a large open barn-type roof. Above the pens was a wooden plank, which allowed the auctioneer to walk quickly round and sell each lot.

A similar process followed when the sheep arrived and they were put into the pens that were on the left of the complex, separated from the pigs by a wide walkway. The process for cattle was more elaborate and a stone-built complex held the beasts in tough, steel-gated pens. A saw-dusted series of concrete paths led from the pens to a centre ring where the animals could be driven round in a circle by the drover and then returned to their pens. Farmers, butchers and other interested parties sat in raised theatre-style seating in order to watch the parade of animals entering and leaving the ring in safety.

Those who worked at the cattle market were all characters like father. Typical of the helpers was Hubert Howard, a local postman who had also helped father in the 1950s with his donkeys. Ernest Crowe (until his illness), Fred Bendilow, Cecil J Holmes, a local pig keeper who was given the nickname Sherlock Holmes, and Harry Boon who did the auction's backroom administration. The drovers would take it in turns to shoo,

For a number of years David Allott helped out at the weekly livestock market, located behind the Borough Bailiff Pub. The building in the background is the former workhouse. The man in the smock is Cecil Holmes. *Picture courtesy of Dr Arnold Kellett and Tempus Publishing Ltd*

jostle and sometimes physically shove animals into the appropriate pen. One simple rule applied when handling the sale animals; never ever hit one. This was not done out of any real feelings for the animal's welfare but because it would mark the meat and meant that butchers would pay less for it, as they would have subsequent difficulties in selling it.

The auctioneer at that time was Tony Thornton, whose forbears had established Thornton and Linley before the First World War. Tony was a stalwart of the local Conservative Association and lived in Boroughbridge Road, Knaresborough. Tony was a little eccentric and a real character, like father.

One of the most difficult tasks was dealing with the cows, bullocks and the occasional bull that arrived at the auction, and this kind of work was normally reserved for father. Each man handling the bigger beasts had a stick which, in the case of father, also had a small metal protrusion, comprising the 5mm end of a nail, fitted into the stick-end for prodding the more aggressive animals. The sticks were for self-defence purposes and the complex used for housing the bigger livestock also had a number of escape alleys to allow trapped men to get away.

Auctioning started around lunchtime and continued until 2pm and sometimes even 3pm if there were a lot of animals to be disposed of. Afterwards butchers, farmers and a motley crew of hangers-on including father would adjourn to the Commercial Hotel (renamed the Borough Bailiff in 1976), for light refreshments. In the early 1970s, prior to licensing reforms, the pub had a permanent market extension, which allowed drinks to be served until 4pm ostensibly to allow buyers and sellers to chat together. However, it was also an after-hours drinking opportunity for everyone in the town and was extremely popular.

I hated Mondays when father was working because it meant that he would often come home well-oiled from the beer he had consumed after the auction. The drinking was partly fuelled by the stress of dealing with animals that were sometimes downright dangerous, and partly by the money father got paid for doing it!

Knaresborough is still a relatively close community and in the 1970s this was even more so. One Tuesday evening in 1972, Tony Thornton attended the Yorkshire Livestock Auctioneers AGM and Annual Dinner, which was held in York. On his way back into Knaresborough along the A59, the local police van which did a daily midnight patrol, decided to follow him down the High Street, which joins the Boroughbridge Road, near Tony Thornton's home at that time.

After following Tony Thornton's Volvo for over a mile, the driver of the police van, who also had a fellow officer with him, flashed the blue light and sounded the horn, but to no effect. Tony Thornton continued driving. On arriving at his home, and aware that the police were not going to give up in a hurry, he rushed the car into his integral garage at an angle, making it impossible for the officers to reach him without coming down the offside of the car.

Tony Thornton then stood at the driver's side of his red Volvo 144S, which was one of the swankier cars. Every time one of the police officers tried to come down the side and arrest him for suspected drink-driving, he hit them. His major complaint seems to have been that he wanted to consult a solicitor before they arrested him. However, this was 1970s policing and as it was now after midnight the local officers were just not interested. Eventually he was apprehended after reinforcements were called and, it would seem, a bit of a scuffle.

Following his arrest, Tony Thornton was put into a police cell after, it would seem, some persuasion regarding the error of his ways. In the 1970s this was quite a local scandal and as is usual in these matters events relating to them can sometimes be quite farcical.

The police station had a local police orderly called George Preston, who also ran a popular fish and chip shop based at 17 Kirkgate. Preston looked after the police station's boiler, brought food for the occasional prisoner held in the cells, and did a number of other menial jobs.

Like many people involved in routine work, Preston was always on the look out for a little bit of juicy gossip to brighten his day. So when

Preston, a former police officer, learnt what had happened, he could not wait to pass the information around the town.

The police orderly and fish shop owner was friendly with Alan Rhodes, who had a little engineering workshop on the other side of the road to the fish shop. Alan was a good friend of Maurice Mapplebeck, who drove the cattle wagon. Maurice was a friend of father's and nearly all the butchers and farmers who frequented the local auction. By the start of the weekend virtually everyone associated with the auction knew about what had happened to poor Tony Thornton – and a number found it extremely funny.

Meanwhile, at around 6.30am on the Wednesday morning, Tony Thornton was released back into the community following the intervention of his solicitor, but not before being charged with drink-driving.

By the following Monday everyone who attended the weekly auction was gossiping about what had happened the previous week. Some of the less informed speculated as to whether Tony Thornton would still be in police custody. Would he arrive in handcuffs? Would a temporary auctioneer be drafted in? Would the auction go ahead at all?

At 11am sharp, Tony Thornton appeared publicly in the cattle market yard, having started his work in the back auction office at 8am, still sporting the remains of a black eye. Some people at the auction felt sorry for him while others thought he had been brought down to size. Father's own view was that he had been stupid trying to hit the police officers and had been given his just desserts.

As Tony Thornton walked along the plank leading towards the sheep, one of the rather boisterous farmers shouted out in front of the crowd of meat buyers and farmers gathered to either bid or simply observe the proceedings: "Come in convict 99, your time is up!" The entire auction crowd, including father, fell about laughing, something which continued for a few minutes. In fairness to Tony Thornton, he took it all in his stride and in true British stiff-upper-lip style, got on with the auction.

Father continued helping there until the 1980s when a series of kicks from the cattle, and arguments with the auction management caused him to hang up his droving stick for the last time.

The incident had little impact on Tony Thornton's career and he went on to become the Vice Chairman of the local Conservative Association and moved sometime later to an impressive new home on the edge of Knaresborough.

Chapter 28

Making Winter Money

Generating money during the winter period was always a problem for father and he would spend large amounts of time dreaming up new ideas. This caused him to develop a whole range of manic schemes, most of which came to nothing.

One of the biggest of these ideas was his plan to create a pet graveyard and crematorium. His idea was to build this on land on the edge of Knaresborough adjacent to the low bridge and Mother Shipton's public house. But he had ignored the fact that the site was under the cliff and part of the local designated conservation area, and that people might just be offended by the smoke and fumes.

Father would discuss with family members for weeks the type of chimney the crematorium would require and how his pet burner would work. The eventual final design comprised four steel corrugated sheets left over from the old wartime Anderson shelter, a metal drainpipe and a large metal grill. The basic nature of this design does not bear further comment.

The outline idea was that he would build a hut on surplus land at the side of the low bridge, where he could receive dead cats and dogs. Owners would be given a choice for their pets of a straight burial, cremation or a combination of the two. For hours he would repeat the words 'frying tonight', much to the irritation of the family. As usual with father's more eccentric ideas, the only people he consulted were those more likely to agree with him and not surprisingly when the authorities learnt of father's idea, they were horrified.

The dreaded Harrogate Borough Council wrote to him and advised him that they would prosecute on environmental grounds due to the pollution issues and a large list of other related offences. He was furious and blamed it all on the small-mindedness of the council's officers. And he never took account of how the public would have reacted to his plan.

Not long after this he hit on yet another big idea, which comprised building a set of donkey racing sulkies. For those not familiar with the term sulky, these are small metal running traps comprising two sets of wheels, a frame, running board and a set of shafts all designed for pulling at high speed by a horse or donkey.

For hours father would puzzle over how the device could be built at minimum or preferably no cost! Eventually, the solution to this problem was found through an unexpected quarter. A big local shop in Starbeck had, for many years, offered a carrier-bike delivery service to nearby residents. Changes in local shopping trends had by the late 1960s rendered this service redundant (funny how things go round in circles). By 1970, 15 bikes had been dumped at the back of the store and were starting to rust. Word of the bikes eventually spread to father who, after some haggling, was able to purchase them all for just five pounds!

Work on converting the bikes into little 'trotting sulkies' (two-wheeled carts) started with great enthusiasm and within a few days father had perfected a prototype. The problem of joining two bikes together was solved using old metal gas pipes and a self-threading spanner-type device. The spanner put a thread on the pipes and allowed them to be screwed into the holes on the top of each bike that formerly held the saddle and handlebars.

For weeks father raved over how sulky racing would replace donkey racing and how this represented the future. After some months the doubt started to creep in about the project. For starters nobody had worked out how the bulky carts could be transported to each event. Putting them into the cattle wagon was a non-starter because the space was needed for the donkeys. After further deliberations the idea was quietly ditched and to my knowledge the bikes are still in the gutter at the back of his old workshop on Harrogate Road, where father dumped them.

Finding extra money especially at Christmas, was always a problem for father, but just occasionally one of his odd ideas would sometimes pay off quite handsomely. One such successful idea was a decision to make up sets of horse brasses mounted on a leather-strap. Father, using his excellent leather working skills, made up ten sets and took them round the various antique shops which, in years gone by, were as prominent in Knaresborough as charity shops are now.

To give the horse brasses 'a history', father painted them all with vinegar in order to tarnish the brass and to give the impression that they were all vintage items that he had found in his loft. Various antique dealers were approached but no one seemed interested. Some shops wanted a more matching set, whilst others wanted a more elaborate mounting. Somewhat dejected, he spoke to a local landlord who surprisingly bought a pair. Father then visited a number of pubs and eventually sold ten sets to a well-known pub near the river, which to my knowledge has some of them still on prominent display.

At this stage having already sold all his stock, he needed to make up further sets and promised the landlord that he would return with them later in the week. Sometime later and four pints heavier, he got up to leave. At this point the local landlord said rather dryly (typical Yorkshire): "Just one thing David, don't bother putting any vinegar on the others as it takes me ages to polish it all off!"

One of the more novel money-raising ideas he hit on was catching and selling river eels. He would brood over his ideas for many months before making a move. In the case of the eels, he worked out the theory but typically had failed to do the necessary research.

His first move was to build some holding cages which he manufactured out of old rabbit hutches and bed irons – the latter are metal strips that were used for the spring part of pre-war beds. The sides of the rabbit hutches were removed and replaced with wire mesh and spring lids were attached using the bed iron. Once the cages had been assembled they were taken down to the little stream that runs between the two Harrogate Road fields for digging in.

The basic theory was that eels would be caught from the River Nidd and then held in the eel cages pending their sale. The fact that nobody might want to purchase river eels had never really entered father's head!

To catch the eels, he put a number of traps into the river and secured their location using flesh-coloured rope. The traps were bated with rotten (smelly) meat and then dropped into the river on the car park side, on the opposite bank to where the donkeys gave rides during the summer. The location was near a place called 'Cherry Tree Deep', so called because of its depth. Some people say that it was created by a boulder during the ice age, others by a freak of nature. All that can be said in respect to the hole is that one of the employees at Blenkhorn's boats once tied three punting sticks together and could still not touch the bottom. Sadly, Cherry Tree Deep is still treacherous and over the years continues to claim a small number of innocent lives of divers, who have become too inquisitive.

Phil Wainman's services were secured to keep an eye on the eel traps; this comprised checking them daily and reporting to father anyone poking about or messing with them. After checking the traps for around three weeks it became apparent that the eels were not interested in playing ball.

Whether he was using the wrong type of bait or trying to trap them at the wrong time of year nobody knows. Like many of father's get-rich-quick schemes, the idea was dropped and the traps were discarded alongside the bikes, behind one of his donkey sheds.

One of the more successful ideas was *B&D Branding* (Betty & David Branding). In the early 1970s horse theft was on the increase and people were genuinely concerned as to how they could protect against their stock being stolen.

He again turned to his life-long friend Jack Barrass, who by this time was a travelling van salesman for George Morrell and sons. Jack's job involved attending the various weekly livestock auctions and selling different items of animal medication such as worming pills. Jack said he knew of a supplier who could provide bespoke branding equipment that could be customised into the animal owner's name. The iron could be supplied with the initials of the owner, which after heating on an open fire could be burnt in at the top of the animal's hooves. No pain is involved and although the branding will eventually grow out and be cut off as and when the hooves are trimmed, the branding gives clear identification for up to 12 months.

Contact was made with the mail order company and within a few days 'hey presto', *B&D Branding* was launched. A number of small adverts were placed in the *Hare & Hounds* and *Yorkshire Life* and father sat back to let the orders roll in. Initially a number of irons were sold, but sales started to drop away once everyone had bought an iron. Within a matter of months mother and father had exhausted the market. However, at least on this occasion the business venture made them a profit!

Father always admired the gypsies who, despite having very little money, could always come up with a money-making idea. One of the services some of the poorer gypsies offered was unblocking drains. He hit on the idea of doing the same using his old chimney sweep rods – yet another money-making idea was born.

Shortly afterwards, the connecting box leading to the main sewer outside Park Place became blocked. Eager to demonstrate to the family his new-found skills, he whipped off the cover-plate to inspect. The connecting box was blocked with five foot of solid sewage that was horrendously smelly. Still not deterred, he began pushing and shoving on his rods but made virtually no impact.

Raymond and I were then called out to assist him. During this intervening period he started shouting and swearing at the neighbours (who were innocent) about their alleged mucky ways – the laws of libel prevent me saying more!

The noise of our heaving and pushing caused such a commotion to nearby residents that one of my teenage school friends who was having a driving lesson, became so engrossed in our activities that he ended up driving down the footpath on Park Crescent. This was much to the annoyance of his own father, a well-known local councillor at the time, who was giving the lesson.

Exhausted and still no further forward with unblocking the drain, father, Raymond and I retreated indoors for a mug of warm coffee. The fact that the lid of the sewer was left off would not normally have been a problem, but for one minor detail: the day in question was a Saturday, the day the milkman called for his money!

Suddenly, and without warning, there was an almighty crash as the local milkman, complete with a tray of empties, fell into the sewer. Rushing out, Raymond and I were faced with the unenviable task of pulling out the milkman who was now covered from head-to-toe in horrendously smelly slime. Frankly, we did not know whether to laugh, cry or run away, but in the end opted to clean him up.

After washing him down for 20 minutes at arm's length with buckets of cold water, whilst the milkman threatened legal action and much more, he was eventually sent off home to change. Thereafter the milk was delivered and money always collected from the Allotts' front door.

Father decided that drain cleaning was yet another job that he was unsuited to perform and this project, like the others, was quietly scrapped.

Chapter 29

The Donkey Cart

For some time during the early 1970s, father felt his business was incomplete without a donkey cart. So in 1972 he bid for a small donkey cart at Appleby Fair but was unsuccessful. Although disappointed over his failure, father hit on the idea of building his own cart and the even better idea of giving the completed cart to Raymond as a birthday present.

To get the project underway a pair of old horse shafts was sent off to William Brear, (see chapter 30) one of father's old friends whom he had known since he had been in his twenties. Bill owned a family sawmill business, called William Brear & Sons Ltd, which was based in a small village called Addingham, near Ilkley, West Yorkshire. At no charge to father, Bill kindly cut the shafts down to the required size and sanded them.

An old small trailer-base was purchased from a scrap yard and some second-hand plywood was donated to the cause by another of father's friends. Assembling the donkey trap took place in father's little workshop in the top field of the Harrogate Road site. A couple of weeks were devoted to the task, with each piece of wooden panelling being carefully cut to shape and interlocked by father. Various pieces of ironwork were purchased from Henry's, the ironmongers, as well as from Alan Rhodes, who owned a small lock-up workshop in Kirkgate.

Meanwhile, a black, second-hand, set of harnesses had been purchased some years earlier and during the evenings he now set about refurbishing them, finishing the job after around ten days of sewing.

During the day work progressed on the cart assembly and within a couple of weeks the task was completed. After assembly the cart was stained a dark teak colour and varnished, then the shafts and the wheels were painted yellow. Some new metalwork was also attached to the shafts and following the fitting of a new wheel tube and the carrying out of a few last minute adjustments, the cart was ready for testing.

A large Irish donkey called Sue had been allocated the task of towing the cart and after catching the poor thing he put her harness on. The donkey was then backed into the cart and a mini-test took place during which a few harness adjustments were made, to ensure Sue would be comfortable.

Most people would have been happy testing the donkey and cart on

The donkey cart was built by father at the height of the 1970s petrol crisis. Picture shows the author Philip holding the reins, with Katherine and Raymond looking on.

Harrogate Road, but he had other ideas. The donkey, father and me trotted off to the Gardeners Arms at Bilton. After a two-hour visit during which father enjoyed a few beers, it was time to trot home. On the way back the donkey, keen to get home, trotted along like a racehorse.

This created quite a bit of interest and resulted in a number of gawping motorists. Those who got too close sometimes got a scowl from father and for the more extreme cases there was even a flick of his horsewhip!

Father had always been a morbid person and after a few days he told me that one of the reasons he had built the cart was for his own funeral. He then went on to explain how if two wooden poles were put across the cart it would carry a coffin. At the age of 13 I found the entire thing totally depressing. Equally depressing for Raymond was the fact that father fell in love with the cart so much that he would not allow my brother to use it, despite the fact that it had been promised to him as a birthday present!

After all the time he had devoted to building the donkey car, father was keen to get some public recognition. An opportunity arose to do this later that year after he agreed to help Father Christmas. Like many of father's promotional ideas at the time, it involved the George Hotel. So on Boxing Day 1974 he took the donkey and cart to a special children's party.

The event had been organised by the pub's darts team and they contributed by buying presents for the children. These were placed in the cart and handed out by Father Christmas, or more accurately John Leeming, who worked at the Dropping Well Estate. This resulted in publicity in the Knaresborough Post in early January 1975 and a follow-on story in the Evening Post. Father, always wary of getting the taxman excited, decided that his three children should front it. At around this time there was a mini energy crisis and so the papers ran such headlines as 'Donkey Sense, at 5-miles-a-carrot who needs petrol?'

In the *Evening Post* a more concise article read: "A Knaresborough man is leading the save-energy campaign and beating the rising price of petrol – thanks to carrot power. When Mr David Allott's three children want to go anywhere he gets out the smart cart he has just built, harnesses Sue, one of his 21 donkeys, slips her a carrot and off they go."

Needless to say, not for the first or last time, all three of us faced a great deal of joking and ridiculing from our school friends after the paper had published the story.

After this initial publicity father got quite excited about the cart and offered it as a complementary fund-raising attraction at donkey derbies. This resulted in the cart being regularly shunted into one of the cattle wagons, for transporting to the various race events the donkeys were attending. Whenever father was involved in the logistics there was always a lot of panicking and shouting. "Steady lad, steady lad you'll damage it, careful, careful don't be so flaming rough." On and on father would chunter until the cart was loaded or put away.

By the mid-1980s Sue was getting too old to pull the cart and after some rudimentary training, a new donkey was given the role. This one had a major defect when it was put under stress but it was not discovered until it was nearly too late. In 1986 the Knaresborough Rotary Club had a donkey derby in the town.

At this time Cllr George Cook was the local Mayor and his wife Doreen was Mayoress. The Cooks had been friends of the family for many years and father was keen to show off his new donkey. The Mayor and Mayoress were duly put into the back of the cart, after which he clicked at the donkey to move it on. However, the donkey had other ideas and refused to budge. Father, slightly irritated, got out his whip and gave the donkey a gentle tap. "Walk on now walk on now," repeated father in a commanding voice, anticipating some action. Suddenly the donkey panicked, but instead of going forwards it went backwards and the more father shouted at it the faster it went – but still backwards.

By now the Mayor and Mayoress were feeling sick and also a little nervous. However, father was becoming more concerned as the back of the cart was now only 30 feet from the front of the cattle wagon and was aligned to hit its steel bumper bar in around 30 seconds.

"Stop, stop you bastard," yelled father as he envisaged his preciously-crafted cart being smashed into matchsticks. Hearing the commotion and shouting, local people stopped and turned and wrongly assumed that he was shouting at the town's first citizens. Fortunately, and without warning, the donkey slowed and then stopped. Three people quickly left the cart in a massive hurry, the Mayor for the toilet, the Mayoress for a brandy and father to be sick.

Father was nobody's fool and after this incident he rather wisely never put the same donkey into the cart harness again. He did, however, continue using the cart – predominately for his own enjoyment, until his premature death in 1993.

Chapter 30

Donkey Racing with Bill

Over the years the donkeys attended a large number of events throughout the north of England. The majority of these were donkey derbies and they followed almost the same pattern, typically comprising eight races with seven or eight donkeys in each race, as outlined elsewhere in this book.

However, just occasionally a donkey derby would stand out from the crowd and be very different. One such occasion was a derby that father's old friend William Brear had organised for one of the various charities he supported.

As mentioned in the previous chapter, father's association with Bill spanned back many years to racing jobs father had done when he was in his prime and the two often joked about bygone times.

Most winters, father lent Bill a donkey called Dandy, a black frisky thing that suffered from bad nerves. Originally, father had assumed that the donkey had been borrowed for a grandchild but as time progressed, it became apparent that Bill's real motive was to annoy some of the local neighbours who had upset him, with the donkey's persistent braying.

They had a far closer relationship than that of father's typical donkey derby organiser. This it would seem had come about after father had got drunk and told Bill that unless he saw a doctor immediately he was going to die. Bill heeded father's advice and, on having a medical check-up, the doctor discovered that he had some kind of ulcer, which if it had not been treated would have killed him.

Father's status as a fortune-teller thereafter, was greatly enhanced and whenever father saw Bill's wife Lillian, she would always consult him at length about the future. Sadly, father could never tell fortunes unless he had been drinking because otherwise he was always too stressed. Over the years this caused all sorts of problems because father was never tactful even when sober!

The donkey derby that Bill had helped organise on this particular occasion was held in a field adjacent to Bolton Abbey, which is located just off the A59 between Skipton and Harrogate. To the best of my knowledge the event took place in 1974 to raise money for the local Lions. One of the reasons that father and Bill got on so well was because Bill was more outrageous than father, as this particular donkey derby was to prove.

The donkeys generally trotted into the wagon with no difficulties

On arrival at the event, Bill came over to greet father and to inform him that a special tent for donkey owners had been erected that would serve them all with beer during the day. Technically, this was for people who had sponsored a donkey in each race, but Bill said because father had brought all the donkeys this was to be his and Bill's own special tent. The tent had been equipped with a counter, crates of bottled Green Label beer and draught Samuel Webster's ale, which in those days were all produced at the Fountain Head brewery in Halifax. Given the small size of the tent it seems unlikely that many of the sponsors were able to fit in, even if they had known about it!

Just as father and Bill got stuck into their first pint, a rather dapper man turned up in a suit, and promptly produced a card advising the wayward pair that he was from Customs and Excise. The bloke went on to say that he was unhappy with some of the day's arrangements as he believed that there was a deliberate attempt being made by the organisers (i.e. Bill) to avoid paying any betting duty. This was actually quite true because he had discovered that if the donkey derby had a tote run by helpers and the donkeys were numbered randomly after the tote had closed, it was treated legally as a game of chance and therefore there was no obligation on the organisers to pay duty.

Rather than listening to what the customs man had to say, Bill told him that if he did not remove his presence in 30 seconds he would have no alternative but to plant him one! Even father was shocked and told

Bill that maybe he ought not to be too hasty. However, Bill was not in the mood for taking advice from anyone and the gentleman was virtually thrown off the site.

This was a bad start to the proceedings and father envisaged more trouble from the authorities, police, Inland Revenue or Customs and Excise later in the day, fortunately however, this did not happen.

The donkeys, which by now were fully tacked up, arrived at the start on time and proceeded to perform well during the first race. This seemed a good start and the young helpers along with myself relaxed with a can of coke each, before the second race.

Suddenly, out of the blue Bill and father came tearing across the field to say that they had just realised that Bill had sponsored a donkey in the second race and they wanted me to ride it. In 1974, I was aged 14 and frankly, this was not want I wanted to do. However, after heavy pressure from Bill and father I reluctantly agreed to ride.

My chosen donkey was Jerry, the 12 hands former Stallion, who was the fastest, but also one of the most difficult donkeys to ride. It may seem strange in today's safety conscious culture, but I preferred to ride without a riding hat, as this is the way father had taught me. At donkey derbies, the jockeys always wore smart racing colours, and hats even in 1974 were mandatory. Therefore, the option of me riding without a hat was a non-starter.

The donkeys raced round a horseshoe shape and a few minutes before the off they would be lined up at the start. Father's rubber starting tape was pulled over the start and the donkey lads would often spend quite a few minutes lining up the more frisky donkeys. An official would hold one end of the tape and in due time the commentator would solemnly announce over the public address system, "Donkeys now under starter's orders." This was always a stressful time because the minute the tote had closed the donkeys needed to be numbered up.

Togged out in racing colours, black riding hat and a grumpy face that would have frightened even a troll, I dutifully took my place alongside Jerry and climbed onto his back at the appropriate time.

Most of the jockeys had been supplied by Harry Fawcett, who was the rather dapper proprietor of the Shadwell Riding School and father's favourite provider. Harry ran a very smart but expensive school for children living in the posh areas of Leeds. Harry was also gay and was nearly always accompanied by his business partner Peter. Whilst father may have had many shortcomings in the way he treated people, he was not homophobic and liked Harry for his horsemanship and the quality of the jockeys he provided. Wherever possible, he would promote the Shadwell Riding School to the various derby organisers.

Riding against good jockeys and on father's most powerful donkey

This was taken in West Yorkshire sometime in the 1970s. Maurice Mapplebeck can be seen cheering in the background next to donkey number 6.

was not my favourite way of spending Saturday afternoons, especially following the lecture I had just received from father about having to win. However, what he had not told me was that Bill had bought the all-winners silver cup that would be presented in the final race and he was desperate to win it back!

Within a couple of minutes, the starting tape had been released and the organiser was waving his flag. Jerry pulled all over the course, cutting up other riders and doing the odd bit of bucking. As we reached the U-bend of the track, Jerry suddenly bolted to the left whilst my body and hat went to the right. The hat fell to the floor and I slipped sideways towards the ground. Realising the massive trouble that I would be in with father if I did not win, I managed to straighten myself up, pull the donkey hard to the right and give it a kick with my heel. Miraculously, I think Jerry realised that he would also be in trouble with father and he rose to the challenge and bounded off after the other donkeys. Using his long legs, Jerry ran at top speed and within a matter of minutes he had overtaken all the donkeys and, fortunately for both of us, we had won the second race.

Winning the second race meant that Bill qualified for the all winners last race and as can be imagined he was cock-a-hoop. Somewhat relieved, I relaxed a little and contemplated whether I could actually win the final race.

Buoyed-up with my success in winning, father and Bill went back to their private tent to continue drinking. To clear my head I went for a look round some of the fund-raising stalls, most of which had been located around the perimeter of the field. These included a variety of children's rides, brick-a-brac stalls, plant stand, café area, large bar, a police car and fire engine plus a stand selling spit roast beef. My recollection is still very vivid about the delicious taste of the roast beef, and it did much to distract me from worrying about the last race.

After what seemed like an eternity, the last race came round and again I was required to change back into racing colours. At this point, the donkey lads took it upon themselves to lend a helping hand, which manifested itself at the starting line. The sombre voice trumpeted out from the tannoy: "Under starters' orders, under starters' orders." Once again, I clambered aboard poor old Jerry.

When the tape was released only one donkey ran forwards and that was mine, because the helpers were holding all the other donkeys back. Needless to say, Jerry bounded round the track and won by a massive lead. At this point, the crowd got aggressive and started shouting: "Fix, fix, fix." Most people would have got upset at the jibes, but not Bill or father.

Delighted with winning back his own cup, Bill stood on the podium and duly received back the trophy he had handed over to the other organisers only a few hours earlier in the day. Father dutifully watched nodding his head in approval as Bill was presented with his winnings.

Bill's favourite tipple was Guinness and on winning the cup, which was capable of holding at least three pints, Bill had it filled with the Irish black liquid which he then passed round his friends. As the winning jockey, I was virtually forced by Bill to drink it despite my protests that I didn't (then) like Guinness.

The end of the event followed pretty much the same format as the other donkey derbies. Father rather drunkenly went off to collect his fee for bringing the donkeys whilst the staff put the donkeys into the back of the cattle wagon.

Within the space of around 15 minutes, all of the donkeys had been put into the cattle wagon. With father now firmly plonked in the front of the cab, the vehicle was soon heading out of the field's main gate.

Starting to doze, father said in a somewhat drunken stupor to Maurice the driver: "Bill really knows how to organise a donkey derby, couldn't fault a thing, first class event. Did you hear those people cheering when our Philip won, really nice people!"

Chapter 31

Getting Older

As the Allott children got older, so their requirements and needs changed. Most of the time father pretended that we were still pre-adolescent, primarily because it made his life easier. This was one of the main reasons why father was still playing Father Christmas to Raymond when he was thirteen!

The world that all three of the Allott children were brought up in was full of contradictions. On the one hand, we were expected at times to behave like adults and sometimes run the donkey business without supervision and on other occasions we were treated like junior school children.

This inconsistency caused all sorts of problems with three teenagers, which subsequently required mother and father to then spend considerable time trying to address. For example, despite our often harsh home life father had strict rules about what Katherine could and could not do. For instance, it was deemed 'un-ladylike' for Katherine to go with the donkeys to derbies and it was not until she was thirteen that father relented. Even then, it was on the strict understanding that Katherine travelled in the front of the cattle wagon, unlike the rest of us who travelled in the box compartment which overhung above the front cab. Another odd rule was that Katherine was not allowed to wear jeans because this is what common women wore (according to father) and she was told that she would not be allowed to wear them until she was 18. To get round this particular problem mother bought Katherine a pair of brushed denim jeans, which father agreed was perfectly acceptable, because he had not seen anyone else wearing them!

When the family was not involved in attending donkey racing or providing donkey rides, we would be taken to the Harrogate Road fields to mess around during the summer months. Mother, who was invariably at work herself, would pack us all up a picnic. Going to the fields to play was provided in compensation by our parents because we did not have a garden. During these slack periods of the donkey business Katherine, Raymond and I would be encouraged by father to play golf at the fields, sunbathe or ride the small Honda motorbike which I had purchased from a school friend. Sometimes we would be taken fishing to Crimple, although we never caught anything.

On one such occasion father got really excited about growing mushrooms and spent weeks cultivating some special spores he had bought from a local shop. After many weeks during the summer and with no results to show, he somewhat angrily tossed the lot onto the manure muckheap outside the stables and then phoned the shop and gave them a good cursing. Whether by divine intervention or by some other means I am unsure, but within a matter of days the muckheap became covered in mushrooms, much to the delight of father who took them all home for consumption!

Another reason for father taking us off to the fields and a slightly more selfish one was that it stopped us meeting up with our mates and being led astray. Friends were always a tricky subject and we always actively discouraged our friends from coming to the house because of its poor state of décor. Often, all three of us pretended that we were not in, to avoid the embarrassment of having to invite people into the house.

As teenagers our main source of information regarding the world was the *Yorkshire Post* that father got each weekday, and the occasional school trip. All three of us saw learning to drive as a great opportunity to leave behind the boring and austere home life and explore new places.

Therefore, as soon as I was 17, I pestered for driving lessons and somewhat predictably, father agreed to teach me. Most fathers teach their children to drive when they are sober, but in dad's case he decided to have a few drinks beforehand so that he could, according to his own account, dull his senses. The first lesson was not a success and he whacked me hard on my left leg with his hand, after I jerked the clutch pedal of his van and caused him to momentarily leave the passenger seat!

Fortunately, once again the good sense of mother intervened. Her solution was to send me off to the Spedding School of Motoring, owned by Malcolm Spedding a nearby neighbour. After a few weeks Malcolm told me to stop driving father's van, because I was developing bad driving habits faster than he could iron them out!

The problem was that father drove in the wrong gears, failed to feed the steering wheel through his fingers and paid scant regard to pedestrians and bikers. He also had a van with defective tracking that caused it to wander on the road. I had also wrongly assumed that doubling your clutch when changing gear and crossing your arms when turning the steering wheel were the required norm!

After about ten lessons with Mr Spedding, father broke his foot and was required to have it put in plaster. He thereafter assumed I was his personal driver and sat in the front passenger seat directing to a variety of pubs in the Harrogate area.

On one such return trip, the old van developed a further fault and the engine started cutting in and out. Father assumed it was my driving and a

Allott children were sent to muck about in the Harrogate Road fields during slack business periods. Note the scruffy attire.

further row broke out. Father made me pull the van into a bus stop so that the problem could be explored. After arguing the toss, he thought that the fault could be a sticking float on the carburettor and so hobbled out of the van and gave it a massive whack with the engine's starting handle. Petrol started to come out of the side of the carburettor, leaving a small pool on the ground. Quickly intervening, I wrapped a rag round the leaking carburettor to stem the flow.

Despite his leg, he clambered quickly back into the passenger seat and lit his pipe to calm his now fragile nerves. As we drove out of the bus stop with the van's engine still cutting in and out, father flicked his still flaming match out of the open window and unfortunately managed to find the spilt petrol. A gush of flames sprung from the bus stop and burnt violently in the air. "At least that's cleaned up the spilt petrol," said father somewhat dryly some minutes later – totally oblivious to the fire engine which was by now passing us on the opposite side of the road, clearly racing to the fire scene!

After a number of months I was relieved to pass my driving test and eventually got permission to drive the van on father's little errands. The sense of freedom this gave me was immense and enabled me to collect turnips and mangles from the Horner brothers, collect the family's weekly meat from Gerald Walker and just occasionally, I was allowed to use the van for attending meetings with my friends. Unfortunately, the van had a number of faults one of which was faulty full beam headlamps, which due to an electrical fault, made them flash like those on a police car. This made it unsuitable for night driving, but because he never used it on an evening, it was not fixed for some years.

As explained earlier, the steering and front tyre tracking were also faulty and this resulted in the van wandering on the road. This problem ultimately resulted in me misjudging the gap between the corner of a house and the road on Waterside and catching the bumper on the house side. In those days, bumpers were made of steel and it buckled out creating a large gap between itself and the van body.

Father accused me of creating a copper's (police officer's) leg trapper due to the bumper straining out. Needless to stay I got a good cursing over the incident before father carefully repositioned the bumper, using a sledgehammer!

Through on-going domestic pressures, I stopped working for father part-time and abandoned the college course I was attending. I then got a job with a graphics company, based on Burley Road in Leeds. Father was genuinely shocked that I did not want to work within the family business and went into a sulk for a number of months. As a consolation I did attend some of the donkey derbies and helped with the odd business emergency until my marriage to Sandra in March 1984.

A few years later, father set about teaching Katherine to drive, in a Ford Thames van. Learning from his earlier mistake with me, father took Katherine off for her lessons on Sunday mornings, with the first one starting at around 7 am. In principle this was quite a smart move by father because it ensured that not only was he sober, but also more focused on the task of teaching. The first lesson by all accounts was a great success and it was agreed that the following Sunday they would start at the even earlier time of 6.30am.

Father's favoured teaching route for Katherine and my own earlier lessons were the farm lanes on the edge of Harrogate, such as the 'B' roads between Harrogate and Follifoot. Father, when he was driving always where possible avoided the main roads because he thought they were dangerous! This attitude stemmed from father's own driving experiences and he would often travel many extra miles to avoid using motorways, 'A' roads and almost any road that had traffic lights. In fact he also hated roundabouts and would invariably get in the wrong lane and then cut up a fellow motorist or worst a biker, as he tried to correct his own mistake.

Over the years his driving got progressively worse due to lapses in his concentration and a couple of accidents where people ran into him. Both accidents involved women drivers and thereafter he assumed (wrongly) that all women drivers, no matter how good they were, were accidents waiting to happen. Looking back, both accidents were unfortunate. The first involved the driver running into the back of his van and banging his head on the windscreen (he always refused to wear a seatbelt) and the second driver did the same thing, straight after he had just had the van repaired from the first accident!

It must therefore be assumed that his attitude to teaching Katherine to drive was, at best, patronising.

On Katherine's second lesson, the telephone rang at home around 8am. Apparently father had grabbed the wheel from Katherine at a difficult T-junction and the van had spun over into an adjacent ditch. Raymond and I were called out to rescue them. Fortunately in the intervening period the local farmer took pity on them and managed to tow the van back onto the road.

From then on, he refused to give Katherine any more lessons on the basis she was dangerous and the task therefore of getting Katherine through her test was given to Mr Spedding and later to the Harrogate School of Motoring.

Not long after passing her test, Katherine got a university offer and departed on her degree course in the autumn of 1984. During the summer months, Katherine would return to help father with the donkeys. After completing her degree in teaching she secured a job in Enfield, settled down, and married Colin Cox.

In 1983, Raymond started driving at the early age of 16. Despite his lack of experience, it seemed safer for him to drive the little sweep van than father, especially after the latter had downed a few pints of beer.

At the age of 17, Raymond did get some professional lessons, although not the amount it would seem Katherine and I enjoyed. Raymond's biggest complaint was that father would leave him waiting for hours outside the Prince of Wales pub in Starbeck, whilst he drank with Gerald and his other local friends. Eventually Raymond passed his test and he bought his own vehicle, a little red mini van.

Father and Raymond had always had a turbulent relationship, primarily because they were very similar (stubborn) and therefore seemed to clash over the same things. As time progressed Raymond took over the sweeping business, but in return had to pay father a financial contribution for each chimney swept.

For various reasons, the relationship between them virtually broke down for a couple of years, which resulted in them not speaking and, not surprisingly, at the age of twenty Raymond moved out. By being extremely hardworking and frugal with his money Raymond managed to buy an elderly house near Harrogate that needed a lot of renovation. Working on the property during the evenings over a number of months, he succeeded in modernising it, which was to be the first of many.

In November 1985 father landed a small radio contract with BBC Radio York. The fee was a modest £20 and it was agreed that he would go on the mid-morning programme to talk about rural history and farming. It was anticipated that he would be interviewed via the Harrogate studio and the whole thing would be recorded in about 30 minutes. After over an hour in the studio and still only partly through his contribution, the controller of Radio York suddenly realised that his contributions could be turned into a mini-series. The programme subsequently ran for many weeks and became popular with many older residents. This recognition gave father a big morale boost, and, at a time when his family had only recently left home, he had a new audience for his story telling.

As time progressed, the relationship between father and Raymond improved and, by the time Raymond was twenty-two, things were back to normal. This culminated in a slightly amusing incident involving father and Raymond, with the former now at the age of 62.

As father got older, he started to enjoy being interviewed by the media. In this picture he is giving a radio interview in Tynemouth.

Father, who had become sick of the constant difficulties of parking on Park Crescent, had taken over from me following my marriage, a small garage at the top of Park Row. The garage was part of a set of eight and could be accessed from an open strip of rough land which connected with Park Row. The garages were on the edge of the town centre and a minority of motorists would sometimes briefly park outside father's garage, blocking his access whilst they collected their partners or went off shopping into Knaresborough!

On this particular occasion, a man in a porkpie hat had decided to park outside the garage. Somewhat aggressively, father told the man in a combination of cusses and two-syllable words to buzz off. The man in question was in his 60s like father and was driving a small mini. Clearly annoyed at father's attitude he lowered his driver's side window and told father where to go.

At this point Raymond appeared on the scene and told the chap in no uncertain language that he should move. When the person in question refused, Raymond simply picked the back of the man's car up and rolled it down the hill on the front wheels. Somewhat shaken the motorist quickly disappeared off, much to the satisfaction of the other two parties. In father's warped world he was very proud of Raymond as he now saw him as someone who would protect him in his old age.

With none of the children now living at home father calmed down in his latter years and took things a little bit steadier. To make life a little easier for himself he purchased a wood cutting bench and reduced the amount of livestock, such as the hens, that he kept at the fields. He and mother also took more holidays (as described elsewhere in this book) and in fits and starts got some of the magic back into their own relationship.

Chapter 32

Illness

Father had been feeling ill during the early part of 1992 and his complexion had changed from its usual red and white, to a greyish colour. The problem had started prior to Christmas when a piece of wood that was being cut on his new petrol driven saw bench had hit him in the stomach and caused him some on-going pain. A visit to the doctor's resulted in some tablets being prescribed, but these did nothing to clear up the discolouring or pain. It was therefore agreed after some further blood tests by his GP that he would go into hospital in March, for a more detailed investigation.

In the period leading up to his hospitalisation father got very stressed. This resulted in my being encouraged to get involved with his business again, including polishing bridles and taking a paintbrush to headbands and even the portable seat. Looking back, this was father's way of coping with his own stress, but at the time I felt I was very stressed.

He was admitted to Harrogate District Hospital and after a series of tests was diagnosed just before Easter 1992 with terminal cancer. The cancer, although small, was blocking his bile duct and this had been why father had gone discoloured. The specialist said it was too dangerous for him to remove the cancer and he therefore inserted a tube bypass to drain away the bile. After he had spent a week in hospital, I was allowed to bring him home. He was very shocked and upset. His main complaint was that he had not had a good crack at the old age pension and that it was all very unfair. I dare say if father had not smoked he might still be alive today, but that is simply conjecture.

It was clear to the whole family that it was only a matter of time before father died and mother, Katherine, Raymond and I were all shell-shocked. Raymond and I arranged a meeting with father's specialist. The consultant said that father could possibly live for a further ten years, but neither Raymond nor I were convinced.

After my marriage to Sandra in 1984, I had managed to avoid getting roped into anything to do with the donkeys, but now things were different and I felt compelled to help. Father, in his stubborn fortitude, was adamant that he would not give the donkeys up, so Raymond and I ran them for the next seventeen months until his passing in late June 1993. Perhaps even more impressive is that our mother who was then in her sixties, ran them from July 1993 until her own death just three years afterwards.

By November, father was still feeling all right and asked his specialist for a further scan. According to the letter received after the scan, the cancer had not grown. However, both Raymond and I remained suspicious. Initially, father was unaffected by the cancer diagnosis and continued as normal. However, as time progressed he started to realise that his days might be numbered and he made a number of visits to family and friends.

One of these visits was to his sister Margaret, whose only contact with mother and father following her second marriage to Herbert Knight had been by letter and the occasional telephone call. In typical style, he travelled down to Minehead in Somerset, where Margaret was now living and working, without telling her in advance.

Fortunately the visit went well and it was at this time that father, on the advice of Herbert, a herbalist, started taking some herbal remedies. His complexion improved and by the summer of 1992 everyone started commenting on how well he looked. In early February 1993, however, he suddenly and rather dramatically lost a number of stones in weight. His face became very gaunt and he and my mother understandably became very concerned.

It was quickly agreed with father's GP that he would be sent to Cookridge Hospital in Leeds for chemotherapy. He began talking about living just a few more years, but by Whitsuntide 1993 that had changed to just a few more months. For father's initial treatment, I took him in my company car. Desperately concerned that the hospital was strictly no smoking, he crammed so much tobacco into his pipe that it overflowed and set the car's carpets on fire!

In those days, Cookridge Hospital had two large wooden tubs at the front of the building into which patients and visitors were encouraged to deposit their cigarette ends before venturing through the entrance door. He was fairly non-committal about the no-smoking arrangements at the hospital and I thought that perhaps, for once, he would be fully compliant. I was therefore somewhat surprised to learn two days later that he was in danger of being expelled from the hospital for arranging impromptu smoke breaks for patients in the main hospital lift. Apparently he had taken a group of patients into the lift and then encouraged them to smoke. The hospital management, on seeing the smoke rising from the lift undercarriage, had wrongly assumed it was on fire and had called the fire brigade. Fortunately, the prompt discovery of the real reason for all the smoke meant that the fire engine could be stood down and returned to its base.

After his brief stays at Cookridge father came home feeling sick and

David Allott with his young grandson Matthew. Note the old buildings in the background which father erected.

would need a few days in bed to recover. Harrogate District Hospital had refused father chemotherapy because the cancer would not respond. Sadly, despite his determination to live, his condition continued to deteriorate and in late May I was horrified to overhear mother telling Alan Dunn that father had only a few more weeks.

By 1993, because of BSE restrictions, it was no longer possible to purchase offal such as pigs' trotters, cows' brains and the like. For someone like father with a farming background, these were delicacies he missed. Typically, father phoned the local butcher and gave him a shopping list. "Sorry David but we're not allowed to sell any of that lot anymore, haven't you heard on the news it could kill you," said the rather pompous butcher.

"Oh that's alright, I am dying already and they don't expect me to see the year out, so it's not really a problem." replied father. The speechless butcher responded quickly and later that day dropped round nearly every item requested by father.

Chapter 33

Racing at Otley

After a break from donkeys which has lasted for more than 10 years I decided, following the onset of father's cancer, to record for posterity a video which would also be a record of the procedures relating to the provision of donkeys by father for derby events.

The event I attended in 1992 was at a school in Otley – which to the best of my recollection was at Prince Henry's Grammar School. The donkey derby was coupled, as were many others, with a children's mini fair.

The day began at around 10am with the donkeys being caught. The rounding-up was achieved using a carrot and stick principle. Wherever possible, the animals were caught using some of the stale bread mother had accumulated over the preceding few days – the carrot. A minority of difficult donkeys, the ones reluctant to be caught, were chased into a corner the fitter helpers and then subsequently held in position by father brandishinig his bulbous stick. A gang of adults and children then helped to put halters on the donkeys so they could walk them down to the front field nearest the lane for grooming.

Father's helpers ranged in age from five to fifty and he had incentives for all of them. There were sweets for the children and beer for the adults, plus pocket money for both, which was aimed at ensuring their services were secured.

The donkeys were groomed using a stiff brush followed by a softer, silkier brush, which was good at removing dandruff. Les Pearson, who provided both father and mother with support during their later years, then proceeded to clean the donkeys' hooves.

The harness required for the event was kept in a converted hen-house located at the top of the second field and was duly brought down in a wheelbarrow to await the arrival of the donkeys' transport, a cattle wagon. The cattle wagon was driven by Jim Brooks who worked for Mapplebecks, the same haulage company which had transported father's donkeys in the 50s.

The cattle wagon would be shunted up the lane, with father's help. This 'assistance' was normally limited to him standing in the middle of the road and waving his stick at any motorist who dared to venture near; and it was woe betide any driver who failed to heed his instructions. On one occasion, he rattled a new car's bonnet causing its nice red paint to crumple. When the driver not unnaturally began to get a little angry, father promptly told him that if he got out of the vehicle he could have some stick as well. And at that, the poor motorist drove off in panic.

Away from the traffic, the helpers would carry aboard the cattle wagon the various items of tack needed for the racing. Included among the bits and pieces were the bridles – each with the name of the individual donkey covered over with red cloth tape and pads with no stirrups (instead of saddles). Much of the harness had been made by father and the reason the pads were without stirrup leathers was to avoid, in the event of an unseating, the jockey being dragged along the ground. A large red notice board with yellow lettering was loaded, proclaiming that these were 'The (famous) Knaresborough Donkeys – available for donkey derbies, galas and related events'. In addition, a large sledgehammer and a 20-yard length of rope for making an emergency pen, racing numbers in black and white for the donkeys and sandwiches for the helpers were put aboard.

It was then time to get the donkeys on board. The first one to be loaded was a rather dim animal called Tony, who had to have his own penned section, because of a habit of lying down in the bottom of the cattle wagon, where he was prone to being walked on by the rest of the donkeys. This particular donkey had to be penned in – and was given a large settee cushion to sit on – while the rest were led into the cattle wagon which was then secured, allowing the helpers to clamber into another vehicle which made the journey behind the donkey transporter.

In the early days of the business, though, it was common for the helpers to travel in the back of the cattle wagon. However, health and safety considerations soon had to be taken into account – along with the dangers of the situation – after some of us sustained injuries. I was among the 'casualties' when I got a bang on the forehead from a steel girder used to separate the animals – and I still bear the skull dint to this day.

The journey to Otley passed without incident with the donkeys arriving on the derby field around noon. Once the cattle wagon was parked, the animals were led out and placed in their holding pen, ready for tacking-up. This process generally took about 30 minutes and woe betide a helper who managed through rough handling to damage any bridle or pad so early in the day.

By 12.30pm father was in urgent need of liquid refreshment and would depart for the beer tent, or the nearest clubhouse or pub. In Otley, it was a nearby pub – although generally he wasn't fussy and it depended on what was open. His disappearance would generally last for a couple of hours, sometimes longer – if we were really lucky!

This event at Otley was typical of the many derbies where father's donkeys raced. There would be a programme of eight races, with eight donkeys in each one. This meant that with 16 animals taken to this particular event, each one would have to race only four times, though even that could prove a little too much for some of them.

The first race at Otley was at 2pm and as soon as the Tote closed the donkeys would be numbered up. Some organisers would have preferred to have the riders – normally provided courtesy of a local riding school – wearing the numbers. But father said he trusted the donkeys more.

A large elastic tape would then be put across the starting line and the jockeys would be encouraged to mount. If everything went according to plan, the jockeys would be of a similar age and weight which in theory gave all the donkeys an equal chance. However, some of the four-legged runners were a little more reluctant than others to actually run – let alone run in the right direction. At some events, some of the riders were so big and so heavy that they literally had to be hauled on to their mounts before the race could get underway.

But when all were aboard and after a quick ready … steady … go … the elastic would twang and the donkeys would set off at a canter or, in some cases a pace more akin to a gentle amble, but hopefully in the right direction.

The secret of riding any racing donkey is not to try to micro-manage it, but let it go with the flow. Even trying to steer the donkey can bring on the onset of a rebellion and cause the rider to lose the race.

After a few minutes, and given a modicum of luck, one donkey at least would reach the finishing post and a result would be announced. Each of the afternoon's races would follow a similar pattern with the event ending at around 5pm.

During the fund-raising day, various sideshows would provide additional entertainment. At Otley, as well as children's games there were bric-a-brac stalls, a coconut shy, a fire engine and a beer tent, though I am not sure if there was any connection between the latter two.

On a good day, father would stay out of the way until at least the fourth race, leaving Jim in the latter days to manage the donkeys and the helpers. On a less fortunate day father would turn up, semi-inebriated and take charge. Taking charge generally meant abusing the helpers and very occasionally walloping a naughty donkey – though there were times when this could be reversed.

Donkey derbies, and especially the four-legged participants, have a knack of attracting eccentrics. On most occasions, this would cause little or no problem. But I can recall that at an earlier donkey derby at Otley a man called Charlie had turned up to do his pantomime piece. This comprised a session of shake-hands-with-uncle Charlie, a 'game' in which his victim – on this occasion my brother – would, when proffering his hand, be picked up and thrown down on top of other youths who by this time were crowding around.

Father, on seeing what was happening as he returned to the donkeys after having a few beers, was somewhat annoyed. The cause of this upset was the grass stains Charlie had created on my brother's trousers, rather than the fact that Raymond could have been hurt. So he decided to play Charlie at his own game. This time when Charlie put out his hand towards father, he found it was he who was picked up – and promptly deposited into a pile of donkey manure. Charlie quickly scurried off in his heavily stained suit and never bothered us again.

There was also a man who accused brother Raymond of stealing his mother-in-law's meat. The cattle wagon driver on that occasion was Maurice Mapplebeck and he and I conferred and decided we couldn't be sure whether Raymond had taken the meat or not. Father was more sure when he arrived on the scene and discovered the meat wedged beneath one of the cattle wagon's wheel arches.

The man promptly began to give father some grief, of the verbal variety, but a quick clip from father cooled him down and put him – briefly – to sleep. Rather embarrassingly, one of the Wharfedale papers took a picture of the man, complete with his mother-in-law's meat, lying prone and with a donkey peering at him from above. The caption read: "One of the donkeys in the derby wonders what put this man to sleep. Answer: He found it too hot to stay awake."

True answer: Donkey Dave's fist!

After the racing, the donkeys would be unpadded and led back into the cattle wagon. Once safely on board, their bridles would then be removed, so they were ready to disembark after the short journey home to Knaresborough.

There the cattle wagon would be backed-up to a small iron gate and the donkeys would be encouraged to leave. Tack would be put back into the wheelbarrow, which was pushed up the field to the hen house. While all this was happening, father would smoke his pipe and try to chat with one of the helpers, although sometimes he got it a little bit wrong. He was once caught talking to a tree, though this was an improvement on when he was discovered after a domestic party happily chatting to mother's curtains!

Chapter 34

Mother and the Donkeys

Following father's death, my mother, although under no obligation to do so, decided to continue running the donkeys. Initially she said she was doing it in order not to disappoint those who had made derby and riding bookings, although it quickly became apparent that she was also taking new bookings.

Some members of the family, me included, had grave reservations about mother running the donkeys for a number of reasons. Firstly, she was a diabetic; secondly, she was a slightly frail pensioner; and thirdly, unlike father, she did not have the experience of maintaining the donkeys. However, she took all of these things in her stride and success-fully ran the donkeys until her own death just three years later. A lot of the heavy work was undertaken by Les Pearson, who had previously worked for father and who was familiar with the various systems that he had developed.

Mother's involvement in the business had been very peculiar. In the early days father had not really wanted her involved and therefore her responsibilities had been more on the periphery, doing things like making sandwiches for the helpers or repairing the donkeys racing numbers. However as time progressed mother had got more involved and in the late 1960s she was collecting the money during Bank Holidays and the more busy Sundays at the riverside. But by the mid 1970s, father started collecting the donkey money himself again – or more to the point, got one of his helpers to do the job, and mother's involvement was delib-erately cut back.

So mother's decision to take on new racing jobs when she had virtu-ally no experience must have been a very hard one for her to make. As time progressed, many of the farm jobs, such as building repairs, started to suffer.

Repairing harnesses was a job handed over to me. While I did my best to complete the work on time, I was less than cordial when mother appeared on a Saturday evening at 7pm with a broken bridle that needed repairing by the morning, in time for another racing event.

Despite mother's frail health, she worked hard with the donkeys and possibly made a lot more money than father, primarily because she did not drink the profits away afterwards!

The basic farm work was left to Les Pearson and he did what he could

Betty Allott was an administrator to the Community Health Council – front right. This picture depicts her early retirement on health grounds. However, after her husband's death she went back to work running the Knaresborough donkeys.

to keep the fences maintained and sheds in good order. However, without father around to chase him around, some of the more straightforward farming stuff started to slip and did not get done.

Mother developed a reasonable rapport with the various groups which required the donkeys for fund-raising events, and the lower profit riding jobs were sidelined. In the autumn, the donkeys were lent to farmers as before, but with the subtle difference that the cattle wagon dropped them all off in bulk.

In between running the donkeys, mother also started to rebuild her social life and formed a friendship with the former KUDC clerk George Barnett. By the January of 1996, it looked like mother had got a grip of her life and was quite enjoying herself. In February of the same year, I visited her on Saturday the 17th and we agreed to go together sometime in the following week to look at televisions.

Three days later disaster struck when mother collapsed at the office of local accountant Derek Taylor, a family friend, and died instantly from a massive heart attack. Her death was totally unexpected and sent all three of her children into serious depression.

After the funeral, I tried to pick up the pieces with Katherine and Raymond. While discussions over the future went on I continued to visit and feed the donkeys each day. But then the weather took a hand. A

Kirsty Allott, the author's daughter takes a riverside ride. Note the boats in the background.

sharp, cold spell was experienced and a one-year-old foal sadly died. The animal had been put in a stable by Les Pearson in mid-February. However, its condition, while not deteriorating, had not massively improved but it was something of a shock to discover it dead. And because of the hard-frozen ground, Bartletts, a regionally based slaughterhouse, had to be paid to take it away.

It transpired that no-one in the immediate family wanted to work the donkeys as this would have meant finishing our existing careers. This was a non-starter because it was not financially feasible, as the donkeys generated a negligible income. So a very difficult decision was made to sell most of them. It was agreed that they would only be sold to good homes and that if the owners decided to subsequently sell-on any of them, then the Allotts would have the first right to buy them back.

An advert was subsequently placed in the Yorkshire Post and the donkeys were sold, mostly over one weekend, for around £50 each. By the Sunday afternoon only Timmy and Jack, whom Raymond wanted to retain himself, remained. The farming equipment, harnesses and numerous related items were put into a sale organised by local auctioneer, Jim Johnson, from Boroughbridge. Much of the house contents were also disposed of via the same route. Contact was made with the various people who had booked the donkeys and they were informed that sadly there were no longer any Allott donkeys to aid their events.

This period of our lives was one of the most stressful for the remaining members of the Allott family. I hope readers will forgive me providing just some of this information in order that the book can be completed without too many loose ends.

Epilogue

Death of a Donkeyman

It was almost impossible to see where the road ended and the sporadi-cally-covered gravel car park started. Only the spluttering gravel and the increased dust emanating from under the car wheels confirmed the changeover. I braked suddenly, sending a sudden large cloud of dust into the early evening summer air. As a sun-lover, the hot weather all week should have been a boon. Instead, I had barely noticed it.

The relaxed but worrying phone call from my mother earlier that day confirmed what I had been dreading and paradoxically, after almost two years, perhaps almost hoped for, namely that my father had started his final descent towards death and would die, according to his doctor, within the next 48 hours.

As I got out of the car, tears started to build at the edge of my eyes. Death was something that happened to other people or that you read about in newspapers, not something that happened to your own father and mother, well at least not then.

Briskly I walked towards the house, tears starting to roll down my cheeks, cutting little black lines through the car park dust which had settled on my face. My sister came out of the front door and walked towards me, she started to put her arm round me but I gently pushed her away. We had never been a particularly emotional family; my father had effectively forbidden it. I tried to chat with her as we walked to my parents' front door, but struggled for words. In the end, I just nodded as my sister attempted to bring me up to speed with the events, which had followed my visit the previous day. Eventually, after what seemed like an eternity, but in reality was a few seconds, we reached the front door.

The door, with its small dints and chipped paint, held almost thirty years of Allott family history behind it. Many of the bumps and chips could be attributed to some event, ranging from a donkey's kick, a thump from father's stick to a milk bottle mark caused by the boy who occasion-ally chased me home from junior school. However, none of this mattered now as I pressed the discoloured door handle and walked briskly into the front room.

My father lay on an old single bed, which had been brought down from the guest room by Raymond earlier that week. Surrounded by familiar family mementoes, pictures of donkeys, walking sticks, pipes and the odd bit of harness, he was in what he would have considered the most comfortable surroundings that money could have bought. His very sick body seemed as if it had almost stripped away his remaining dignity, and yet even on the verge of death he still managed to dominate the household, just as he had done all my life.

Talk, beyond the basic pleasantries, had ended the previous week after my father's ability to have a reasoned conversation had deserted him. "Hello Dad, how are you," I started, knowing in my heart that he was a lot worse than the day before. No answer was forthcoming and I realised that either he could not hear or did not want to devote what meagre life energy he had left to making some kind of reply – polite or otherwise.

My mother was standing beside the bed and waiting on father's every wish. Looking round the room reminded me of much happier days. The Christmases the family had spent together in the same room, the fun and also the sadness the room had shared with us all.

The sweet smell from father's pipe had until recently wafted freely around the same front room since the 1960s. Although father had now abandoned his pipe for good, the discoloured wallpaper in each of the corners of the back room still bore testimony to his love of the pipe.

I left the front room and walked into the living room, visibly upset by my father's condition and unable to cope with the emotions of seeing him almost helpless like this. My sister Katherine, who had gone into the living room on my arrival, seemed a little more composed than me about the rapidly deteriorating situation.

A knock at the door sent my sister scurrying to see who was calling and Dr Walton entered. Father was now part of the doctor's nightly round and Katherine brought him into the living room as a prelude to his seeing father. "What's the precise situation doctor?" I asked anxiously. "Well," said the doctor, "Your father will die this evening or tomorrow. Frankly he should have died weeks ago but then, as you know, he is a very tough bloke."

Contemplating life without father was impossible. Despite running it through in my mind for month after month, sleepless night after sleep-less night, it was impossible to know what it really would mean. A further knocking on the door interrupted our conversation as the Macmillan nurses arrived. The nurses had been coming each evening for a week and had been wonderful in relieving my mother of some of the more basic and unpleasant tasks associated with father.

The conversation with Dr Walton never resumed and, confused and disturbed by the depressing atmosphere my former home had taken on, I decided to leave. With hindsight I should have tried to kiss father, but given his attitude earlier in the week when I had tried to comfort him by attempting to play with his hair and father had reacted by brusquely trying to push me away – I thought better of it.

Looking round the front room door, I said goodbye to father, as the Macmillan nurse tried, without much luck, to get him to put on a fresh pair of pyjamas. Earlier that week two nurses had visited and both had received a good cursing from father for attempting to boss him around. In a warped sort of way, it had been quite amusing, and the well-meaning nurses had certainly met their match.

"Are you as rough with all the old bastards you have to deal with, don't be so bloody rough" spat out the old man. The nurses had patiently not said anything in retaliation on that Wednesday, and they certainly treated him now with a knowing respect.

I left the house and walked to the car. Despite the time, the car seats were still hot and I slightly burnt the back of my legs as I got in. On arrival at home I helped myself to a large whisky and brought Sandra my wife up to date with events arising from the visit. After further drinks and a light supper, I retired to bed, sufficiently inebriated at least to sleep. Sandra climbed in after me, although I had little recollection of this, as I dropped almost immediately to sleep.

At around 12.30am the telephone rang, an unusual event in the normal scheme of things but not, given the evening's events, altogether unexpected. Bleary-eyed I answered. Mother said: "I am just phoning to say that your father died quietly in his sleep 10 minutes ago. He held Katherine's and my hand and died peacefully as he had wished."

The tears that were in my eyes earlier returned and I asked mother if she wanted me to go up. "No Philip, we will need your assistance in the morning and need you at your best, so please can you come up then?" I rose early for a Saturday at 7.30am, and, after washing and dressing, consulted the York *Yellow Pages*, while Sandra, who had got up at the same time, prepared some breakfast.

As with everything involving father, even in death matters were not going to be easy. He had laid down strict instructions that he wanted taking to the cemetery on his donkey and cart, a wish which despite pressures from relatives to the contrary, I was duty-bound to honour. Finding an undertaker who could take responsibility for this little lot was not easy, but by the end of my *Yellow Pages* search, I had identified at least a trio of potential funeral directors.

After breakfast I drove up to mother's without really knowing what to expect. Remarkably, she and Katherine were quite composed, although clearly very subdued. The doctor had already been and signed a death certificate so at least that formality had been completed.

I said to mother that I wanted to take a look at father and walked into the front room. His sick body lay on the bed. His eyes were wide open and his face was expressionless. This image of father shocked me to the core, although in a strange way it was also reassuring.

His body devoid of all energy seemed so empty and, if I may say, was soulless. This confirmed in my mind that father's vitality and energy must have gone somewhere and that he had moved on to another world. After looking at him for a few minutes, I left the room. Some people talk to dead bodies, but father's was so empty that it seemed pointless.

I set to work on the telephone calling potential undertakers. The first was going on holiday and could not help, but the second was more than amenable and agreed to come straight away. The undertaker, Mr Fred Scatchard, arrived in a white, unmarked van. It turned out he was a friend of father's and after a few minutes discussion I led him through into the front room.

"Why the poor bugger," he said: "I only saw David around 12 months ago and he looked fine then."

"That's what cancer does for you," I mumbled back. "Do you need any help with him?"

"No, that's OK. I've got one of the lads in the van, please leave it to us," replied Mr Scatchard.

Somewhat relieved, I retired to the living room. Watching from the window, I saw Mr Scatchard beckon to a young man from the front door. The young man got briskly out of the front of the van and then, stopping at its rear doors, removed a standard, light white plastic coffin.

After a few minutes in the front room both men left the house when the street was empty, carrying the rather undignified coffin. The next few days were spent arranging the funeral. My employers Greyhound Marketing Ltd owned by Bob and Carol Simpson, had been rather decent about the whole matter and had given me a week's compassionate leave. This gave me an opportunity not only to arrange the funeral but also to reflect on my father's life.

He had always lived a life that was different, if not downright eccentric. For nearly forty years he had kept, bred and raced a troop of donkeys which at times topped 20. Many people believed – rightly – that he thought more of his beloved donkeys than he did of people. Even on the Sunday before his death, he had insisted on going to Bradford to watch his treasured donkeys' race. Unable even to stand, he had taken his own chair.

The arrangements for the funeral ranged from the formal to the most bizarre. It was agreed that the hearse would take him to the Parish church and the donkey and cart to the cemetery. This was all subsequently timed by taking the donkey chosen to pull the cart out on a practice run a couple of days before. People invited to the funeral ranged

Timmy the donkey led father's funeral procession. The number of journalists covering the event, funeral traffic and general High Street traffic brought the town centre to a standstill. Left to right, Eddy Lofthouse, Timmy the donkey, Les Pearson and behind Les, Darren Lofthouse and at the rear of the coffin Darren's friend.

from local dignitaries to gypsies and a reception afterwards was arranged at the Borough Bailiff Inn.

Timmy, a large brown donkey, was given the honour of pulling the cart because of his strength and past experience between the shafts. Erring on the side of caution, I took the donkey and cart on the pre-event run and it became clear that the funeral would create some major traffic headaches and might possibly gridlock the town centre for sometime afterwards. Accordingly, the local police were alerted and it was agreed that traffic would be held back at key points on Knaresborough High Street, in order to allow the funeral cortege to move en-block, so it would not become fragmented.

On the day, the church service went without a hitch. The coffin arrived on time and the vicar, who had been pre-briefed by the family, gave a good account of the many and varied things that father had done during his life.

Knaresborough Parish Church was absolutely packed, which spoke volumes for the friends and associates who had all come to say farewell to Knaresborough's first, and perhaps last, Donkeyman.

After the service the coffin was carefully loaded on to a white board which had been placed over the back of the donkey cart which father had

Fred Scatchard the undertaker walks with the Timmy the donkey and Les Pearson to the cemetery

built all those years ago. The funeral cortège moved off led by the donkey and cart, at a very slow pace.

Seated in the first car behind the cart were Mother, Aunt Margaret, Katherine, Raymond and me. The donkey pulling the cart had never been one of our race-winning animals and now, led by Les, one of father's key helpers, moved very slowly. As we approached the middle of the High Street, my mother, sister and I burst into laughter for a few seconds, conduct totally unbecoming for a funeral.

The reason for these hysterics was the chaos and comical situation that father was causing, even in death. Marching at the front with his top hat and looking very distinguished was the undertaker Mr Scatchard, behind him the donkey and cart, followed by two funeral cars and just about everyone in cars, who had been in the parish church.

The High Street came to a standstill as lorries and cars coming the other way gave way and then found that due to the sheer weight of traffic their route was blocked. Meanwhile on the footpath an assortment of cameramen from television to newspapers, as well as interested members of the public ran amok snapping pictures of the donkey and cart, many of which subsequently appeared in the regional media.

After what seemed like an eternity, we eventually arrived at the cemetery gates. The steel gates, green and battered, had been opened in advance and the cortege moved slowly past those who had been buried in the cemetery many years ago.

The donkey did not take kindly to some of the gravestone colours, and pulled sharply to the right when it saw a white plastic bag which suddenly blew towards the cart from behind a winged angel. The grave, next to father's parents resting place, had been opened earlier in the week. The position of the site was not down to mere luck, but rather to the thrifty if not morbid decision made by father to purchase his own plot many years earlier.

A little tarmac footpath ran along the back of the grave and with a little careful management, the cart was brought along this narrow passage. After the internment, the donkey and cart were led back to the riverside. Mourners followed the two funeral cars to the Borough Bailiff, which had opened its only function room for the occasion. Inside gypsies, relatives, farmers, neighbours, business associates and friends, all told their different stories about David, the Donkeyman.

Drinks, sandwiches and tongues moved fast. Despite the diverse backgrounds of those present, everyone seemed to be engrossed in discussions about father. Mother, Katherine, Raymond and I tried very hard, despite our sorrow, to make everyone welcome.

After fifteen minutes I leaned against the fireplace and took a look around at those present. There was Maurice Mapplebeck, the former cattle wagon driver, who had taken my father and his donkeys all over the North of England. And there, too, was Sharkey, the hard-man gypsy, who drank with father and who had burst into tears when father told him that he had been diagnosed with cancer.

Mother and father's best friends Gerald and Edith Walker, Uncle John and his family from Leeds, the Town Crier Sid Bradley, my friend John Windsor and his sister Ann – they were all among the large number of others present. All had one obvious thing in common; they had known father through his love of donkeys.

Typical of these were Harry and Ester Pearson who had travelled down from Northumberland. They had known father for a number of years through the donkeys he had supplied to organisations they supported like the Tynemouth Scout Association, to raise charity money from donkey derbies.

Thinking about this common link made my mind go back to my own childhood and to how donkeys had played a pivotal part in my life until I was in my early twenties.

Father had run the donkeys from the 1950s as a profit-making venture and people had often travelled great distances to seek his advice or to try and sell him a donkey. Most people in Knaresborough and the surrounding villages knew of Donkey Dave, and his animals had raised large sums of money for charities and organisations across the North of England.

Some of these letters of enquiry from organisers concerning the donkeys sent to father often had the minimum amount of address information. For example 'Donkey Dave, Knaresborough' or 'The Donkeyman, Knaresborough' were not unusual – but still found their way to Park Place!

His outspokenness, strength of character and knowledge of donkeys had made him numerous friends – not to mention enemies in almost equal numbers – many of whom had attended the funeral. The sad thing was that when he was alive, his family loathed him for trying to dominate and organise their lives, but now he was gone we were already missing him.

For the Allott family, Knaresborough, the donkeys and the numerous friends and acquaintances my father had known, and all those whose lives he had enriched, things would never be quite the same again.

Appendix 1: Donkeys & Helpers

Donkeys Roll Call

1 Alice
2 Ann alias 'wooden top'
3 Chloe
4 Daisy
5 Dandy
6 Felix
7 Jane
8 Jack
9 Jenny
10 Jerry
11 Jill
12 Judy
13 June
14 Katy
15 Leo
16 Mandy
17 Mary
18 Muffin
19 Nelly
20 Pat
21 Peter
22 Punch
23 Rosy
24 Sally
25 Sammy
26 Silver
27 Sooty
28 Sue
29 Sweep
30 Tammy
31 Timmy
32 Tiny
33 Tommy
34 Tom
35 Tony

Donkey Helpers Roll of Honour

Philip Allott
Katherine Allott
Raymond Allott
Audrey's two daughters
Jack Bailes
Paul O'Brien
Johnathan Boyes
Graham Burnham
Louise Castleton
John Davey
Mick Dobson
Fred Hawkes
Alvin Hood
Hubert Howard
David Irvine
Alan Jubb
Darren Lofthouse
Eddy Lofthouse
Margaret Mapplebeck
Corrina Graham-Merrett
Kevin Mothersill
Norman Mothersill
Garry Mottley
Les Pearson
John Rabbit
Mary Roberts
David Sheppard
Bob Scurr
Carl Stubbs
Michael Stubbs
Gerald Sutcliffe
Jill Sunley
Andrew Taylor
Derek Taylor
Derek Tucker
Ian Wallis
Tracy Wainman
Vikki Wainman
Gordon Wappett
... and countless others

Wagon Drivers

Jim Brook   Ken Mothersill
Maurice Mapplebeck   Winston Wrechless
Jack Mapplebeck

Local Professional Jockeys

Denis Buckle   Philip Poval
Gordon Davis   Charlie Roberts
Eddy Larkin   Ray Sheather
Geoff Littlewood   Eric Walton
Tommy Miller   Scooby Breezly
Gordon Monk   Bob Scurr
Billy Nevitt

Local Amateur Jockeys

Wayne Aylesbury   Vicki Johnson
Charlotte Brooks   Nicola Miller
Leigh Bulmer   Vanessa Mitchell
Joanne Chadwick   Nigel Pickering
Anthony Clark   Colin Prideaux
Tommy Douglas   Keith Radcliffe
Mandy Gill   Jane Rawlings
Kevin Gray   Julie Schofield
Rae Green   Joanne Taylor
Helen Grundy   Nannette Watkin
Fiona Hemingway   Gaynor Watson

Riding Schools

Murton House Riding School
Shadwell Riding School
Countless others in the North of England

Appendix 2: Events

The Knaresborough donkeys raced all over the north of England in order to raise funds for a variety of different causes and also attended many sports days to give rides. Although this list is far from comprehensive, it does provide an overview regarding some of the locations and fundraising causes. Perhaps you attended one of these events?

Organisation	Date	Event	Purpose
Alnwick RFC	1995+	DD	Fundraiser
Ashington RFC	1995+	DD	Fundraiser
Barnsley District Lions Club	1971	DD	Charity fundraiser
Batley & Birstall Boys Clubs	1975	DD	Fundraiser
Bilton Hall Garden Party	1994	F	Fundraiser
Bingley Lions Club	1965	DD	Charity fundraiser
Bishop Thornton	1975+	DD	St Joseph's Church
Blythe Spartan FO Northumberland	1994	DD	Fundraiser
Boston Spa & Tadcaster Round Table	1980	DD	Charity fundraiser
Birstwith Horticultural Society	1993+	R	Birstwith Show, fundraiser
Bradford South (18th) Scouts	1989+	DD	Fundraiser
Braham, Hargreaves	1962+	R	Staff open day
Bramley Old Boys RUFC	1965	DD	Fundraiser
Brighouse Round Table	1982	DD	Halifax General Hospital
Bolton Abbey	1984*	DD	Fundraiser local Lions
Burton Leonard	1956	R	Village fundraiser
Castleford Lions Club	1975	DD	Fundraiser
Cairsides Farm, Rushyford, Co Durham	1991	DD	Fundaiser
Cleckheaton Rugby Union	1971	DD	Mentally handicapped children
Colne	1964	DD	Fundraiser
Colne Valley	1973	DD	Charity fundraiser
Follifoot	1956	R	Fundraiser
Halifax	1964	DD	Fundraiser
Harrogate, ICI	1962+	R	Children's sports day
Harrogate, Lions Club	1991+	R	Carnival, fundraiser
Harrogate Rugby Club	1967+	DD	Fundraiser
Harrogate, Wheatlands School	1956+	R	School gala
Harrogate, Woodlands School PTA	1962+	R	May Fair
Haverigg Inshore Rescue Team	1995	DD	Fundraiser
Heckmondwike Sports Club	1982	DD	Heckmondwike Scout Group
Honley High School	1993	DD	Fundraiser
Horsforth Gala	1964	R	Fundraiser
Huddersfield New Mill Gala	1993+	DD	Fundraising Gala
Huddersfield RUFC	1964	DD	Charity fundraiser
Huddersfield Conservative Party	1974	DD	Fundraiser
Goldsborough	1959	DD	Fundraiser
Guiseley, Brook Crompton	1994+	R	Factory open-day
Keighley, held at Woodville Road	1964	DD	Fundraiser
Knaresborough Children's Day	1992+	R	Local children
Knaresborough Lions Club	1992+	DD	Charity fundraiser

Knaresborough St John's Flower Fest	1992	R	Fundraising
Knaresborough Rotary Club	1967+	DD	Local charities
Knaresborough Round Table	1970	R	Bed Race, local charities
Leeds, The Cavaliers	1966+	DD	Fundraiser
Leeds Jewish Community	1964	DD	Fundraiser
Leeds, John Smeaton High School PTA	1978+	DD	Charity fundraiser
Leeds West School, evening event	1967	DD	Fundraiser
Manchester, Langley Labour Club	1967	DD	Fundraiser
Menwith Hill (Harrogate)	1967+	R	Independence day 6th July
Ministry of Agriculture	1962	R	Fundraising
Nelson & Colne Conservative Assoc	1965	DD	Fundraiser
Northallerton, Hurworth Hunt Supporters	1990	DD	Fundraiser
Ossett Cricket & Athletic Club	1961+	DD	Fundraiser
Otley Rugby Union Club	1976+	DD	Fundriser
Pannal, Bintex Sportsday	1962+	R	Galaday
Penistone Sports Club	1963	DD	Fundraiser
Penny Sq Army Apprentice College	1995+	DD	Fundraiser
Pudsey	1962	DD	Fundraiser
Richmond, held Kirklevington	1992	DD	Unknown
Rothwell & District Round Table	1970	DD	Charity for mentally handicapped
Queensbury Scout Group	1993	DD	Charity fundraiser
Queensbury Tryhards	1989	DD	Fundraiser
RAOB	1994	R	Garden party fundraiser
RAOB Skipton	1996	DD	Fundraiser
Rawdon	1964+	DD	Charity fundraiser
Rawson Sq Army Apprentice College	1993	DD	Fundraiser
Richmond RUFC	1996	DD	Fundraiser
Ripon City Football Club	1962	DD	Fundraiser
Sedgefield, South Durham Hunt	1991	DD	Fundraiser
Sheffield Young Farmers' Clubs	1969	DD	Fundraiser
Shelley AFC	1962	DD	Fundraiser
Shipley & District Round Table	1971+	DD	Underprivileged Children
Sowerby Bridge	1964	DD	Fundraiser
Spofforth Long Memorial Hall	1959	DD	Renovation Fund
Starbeck Gala	1988+	R	Fundraiser
Thornton District Scout Council	1996	DD	Fundraiser
Tynemouth Scout Association	1992+	DD	Fundraiser
Wakefield Young Conservatives	1962	DD	Fundraiser
Wakefield Sports Club	1972	DD	Nursing staff welfare funds
Wakefield Sandal Rugby Union	1967	DD	Fundraiser
Weeton & District Show	1991	R	Fundraiser
West Leeds Boys School	1976+	DD	Fundraiser
West Riding Ass of Youth Clubs	1962	DD	Charity fundraiser
Wetherby Donkey Derby	1956	DD	Fundraiser
York held at the race course	1967*	DD	Fundraiser

DD = Donkey Derby
R = Riding
+ = Repeat bookings; the date shown will not necessarily be the first event held
* = Estimated date